# BRITISH COLUMBIA
# WILDLIFE
# viewing guide

**BILL WAREHAM**
Principal Author

**GARY WHYTE**
Editor-in-Chief

**SHANE KENNEDY**
Coordinator

BRITISH
COLUMBIA

WILDLIFE
WATCH

HABITAT
CONSERVATION
FUND

LONE
PINE

*The Publisher:*
Lone Pine Publishing
#206 10426-81 Avenue
Edmonton, Alberta, Canada
T6E 1X5

**Canadian Cataloguing in Publication Data**
Wareham, Bill, 1959-
British Columbia wildlife viewing guide

Includes index.
ISBN 1-55105-001-3 (bound). -- ISBN 1-55105-000-5 (pbk.)
1. Wildlife watching--British Columbia--Guide-books. 2. Zoology--British Columbia.
3. British Columbia--Description and travel--1981-  --Guide-books. I. Title.
QL60.W37 1991    591.9711    C91-091415-X

*Front and back cover photo:* Clinton Webb / WCWC
*Front cover inset photos:* Dennis A. Demarchi, Mark Degner,
Wayne Stetski / B.C. Parks, Doug Leighton (top to bottom)
*Back cover inset photos:* Dan Culver (top), Adrian Thysse (bottom)
*Cover and book design:* Beata Kurpinski and Yuet Chan
*Black and white illustration:* Rose-Ann Tisserand and Greg Huculak
*Colour illustration:* Ewa Pluciennik (birds) and Linda Dunn (flowers)
*Mapping:* Rick Checkland
*Printing:* Kromar Printing Ltd., Winnipeg, Manitoba, Canada

# Contents

*Wood duck*
B.C. PARKS / A. GRASS

# Acknowledgements

This book is the result of the combined efforts of many, highly committed individuals. Each of them can take credit for a job well done.

Bill Wareham of Phoenix Environmental Research and Planning Services was the principle researcher and writer. Photo research was conducted by Duane Fortier.

Project management was coordinated by Shane Kennedy and Gary Whyte of Lone Pine Publishing and John Youds of the B.C. Wildlife Branch. Participants associated with Lone Pine's involvement included Elaine Butler, Yuet Chan, Rick Checkland, Diego Gazzola, Brad Hornseth, Phillip Kennedy, Beata Kurpinski and Brian Stephens.

The collecting of information for site descriptions, maps and directions was assisted by many individuals. We would like to thank the following people who contributed information to the project and acknowledge that there were many others who were part of the process. To all of you, our deepest thanks for your support and advice.

Betty Brooks
Tom Burgess
Jim Butler
Ken Child
Brian Churchill
Jim Cuthbert
Peter Davidson
Rick Davies
Neil Dawe
Jovanka Djordjevich
Orville Dyer
John Elliot
Al Grass
Jude Grass
John Gwilliam
Larry Halverson
Jay Hammond

Daryll Hebert
Deiter Hollman
Bob Hooton
Rick Howie
Joyce Hutchinson
Peter Joyce
Doug Jury
Frank Kime
Dave Low
Rick Marshall
Tim Matheson
Ian McTaggart Cowan
Bill Merilees
Don Miller
Daryl Moraes
Nancy Newhouse

Juanita Ptolemy
Ralph Ritcey
Chris Ritchie
Anna Roberts
Gail Ross
Mike Sarrel
Andy Stewart
Terry Sullivan
Robin Sydney-Smith
Brenda Thomson
Syd Watts
Bryan Webster
Nancy Wilkin
Anna Wolterson
Elizabeth Wooding
Guy Woods

Special thanks to John Youds, who provided valuable information and constant support, and to Dennis Demarchi, also from the B.C. Wildlife Branch, who supplied information and direction on the use of ecoregion classifications for the book's outline and chapter headings. We also thank Dennis Demarchi for permission to use the Ecoregion maps.

The production of this book is the result of a cooperative joint venture effort between Lone Pine Publishing, the Habitat Conservation Fund and B.C. Environment. The effort was also encouraged by the provincial Wildlife Viewing and Wildlife Viewing Tourism Committees.

Finally, we thank B.C.'s researchers, biologists, wildlife managers and amateur naturalists who continue to further the work which leads us to a better understanding and stewardship of wildlife in B.C. We encourage everyone to support the valuable work of these dedicated people.

# Preface

British Columbia is an extraordinary province for those who delight in seeing wildlife. We have the greatest variety of habitats of any Canadian province. From the semi-deserts of the southern Okanagan to the alpine tundras along our northern boundary and from the open sea of the Pacific Coast to the Rocky Mountains, biologists have identified ten ecoprovinces with distinctively different assemblages of plants and animals.

It is not surprising that B.C. is home to more kinds of animals than all the other provinces of Canada. The quest to see and identify these species can provide a lifetime of enjoyment. For thousands of British Columbians, every spring brings the excitement of watching for returning migrants — the arrival of old friends.

There is special excitement in glimpsing the large mammals. Moose, elk, caribou, mountain sheep, mountain goat, mule and white-tailed deer can all be seen from provincial highways at one point or another by keen observers who bring patience to the task. Here and there it is possible to see a black bear, coyote or even a wolf.

A grizzly or a mountain lion would be a rare and memorable sighting for they are secretive and generally avoid people.

This guidebook is designed to help you reach places where you are likely to see some of these animals: muskeg or lake shore where moose come to feed morning and evening; a mountain vista where white dots high on the slopes materialize into mountain goats through your field glasses, or a wildlife reserve rich in birds and mammals.

While you are seeking out and enjoying these places, remember to go quietly in the presence of wild things and look about you at the wealth of plants that are the source of all animal energy.

Remember also that this great wealth of living things in British Columbia can only survive if the habitat is maintained intact. It is the responsibility of each of us to see that this is so.

Dr. Ian McTaggart Cowan
Chairman, Public Advisory Board
Habitat Conservation Fund

### Getting the Most out of Watching Wildlife

While this guidebook may assist you in finding many of B.C.'s important wildlife areas, seeking and finding wildlife closely and consistently requires special skill. Choose your viewing times and destinations carefully by thinking through your intentions. A wildlife experience has three stages: anticipation, participation and recollection. If you cut short the first through little forethought, you decrease a trip's full potential.

Although early mornings are invariably the best times for most wildlife activity, you should explore a range of periods, especially late evening and after dark. Sitting quietly for extensive periods in one place makes good sense at water holes where many birds remain high in the evergreen spires, otherwise defying good observation. Use vegetation and even your car as a blind for wildlife viewing. Proper binoculars or a spotting scope are basic equipment today. Be patient, and allow for more time than anticipated. Speak with others about what you are searching for, and share your discoveries. Worthwhile friendships and reciprocal information will often be the result. Take advantage of available facilities, publications, field guides, and interpretive programs.

When in the field, move slowly and quietly. When in close proximity of wildlife keep your actions especially slow, avoiding quick movements. Brightly coloured clothing will also decrease your chances of seeing shy and elusive species. Use your eyes and ears to locate wildlife. If you are searching for particular birds, learn their songs first from one of the many available sound recordings. Do not simply list the species you meet, but get to know them, and think about the behaviours you observe. Keep an on-going notebook of the details and circumstances of your observations.

Most effective wildlife viewing represents simply good common sense. Fostering proper skills will serve as good example for others and provide for yourself a more meaningful and enjoyable experience.

Jim Butler
Professor, Parks, Wildlife and Interpretation
The University of Alberta

---

### The Habitat Conservation Fund

One avenue for conserving fish and wildlife habitat is the Habitat Conservation Fund, the largest broad-based habitat enhancement fund in British Columbia.

By purchasing this wildlife viewing guide, you have already contributed to habitat conservation in British Columbia: some of the proceeds from this book go into the Habitat Conservation Fund where the money will go directly to habitat enhancement projects throughout the province.

The Habitat Conservation Fund was created in 1981 by an act of the legislature to ensure that our valuable living resources continue to be among the most abundant and diverse in North America.

Anglers, hunters, trappers and guides contribute to the Fund's habitat enhancement activities through licence surcharges. The Fund also receives tax deductible donations from individuals, conservation groups, and corporations.

If you are interested in finding out more about the Habitat Conservation Fund or would like to make a donation, contact:

HABITAT CONSERVATION FUND

Habitat Conservation Fund
Wildlife Branch
B.C. Environment
Parliament Buildings
Victoria, B.C.   V8V 1X5

# Introduction

British Columbia's landscape is immense and varied, the best of it still wild. An abundance of wildlife has given the province an international reputation as a wildlife viewing area. This guide is intended as a starting point in the exploration of nature in the province. Use it in conjunction with field guides and natural history books to increase your understanding of the species that you encounter. You may see animals not mentioned here; others may be discovered only after hours of patient, quiet waiting.

This guide is organized into nine terrestial Ecoprovinces using the ecoregion classification system which offers a framework for interpreting the complex interrelationships between landscape, climate, vegetation and representative wildlife species. The province has been divided into 85 units. Placing these in a hierarchical system lets us better understand an area in relation to its local, regional, provincial, continental and global context. Ecodomains and Ecodivisions are very broad in scale and place B.C. in a global reference, while Ecoprovinces, Ecoregions, and Ecosections are progressively more detailed and narrow in their scope.

This conceptual anatomy of the province may help us to be more aware of the environment of B.C.: of which unique ecosystems exist here and how these habitats are connected and interact with each other. Wilderness advocates may use this classification system for putting wilderness proposals into a provincial and global perspective. Wildlife managers use the ecoregions to visualize the broadscale distribution of wildlife in a province where many species make annual, elevational or transglobal migrations. For the amateur naturalist, the ecoregion boundaries assist in better understanding the occurrence of wildlife and in locating species in areas not mentioned in this guide.

Wildlife symbols in this book highlight the more viewable or distinctive species at each site, and contact numbers have been provided for additional information regarding site facilities, access and interpretive resources.

Begin your discovery of British Columbia's watchable wildlife at any one of the sixty-seven sites included here. The guide represents only a sampling of the abundant and diverse wildlife-viewing opportunities to be found throughout the province. The sites contained within this guide were selected from over three hundred locations which were examined for their viewing potential and for their sensitivity to the possible impact that would occur through increased visitor activity.

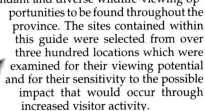

The range of British Columbia's wildlife is beyond imagination. You won't see it all, but what you do discover will be a part of your memories for years.

# Key to Symbols

**Wildlife Symbols:**

 Songbirds

 Upland birds

 Waterfowl

 Shorebirds

 Pelagic Birds

 Other Water Birds

 Birds of Prey

 Small Mammals

 Hoofed Mammals

 Carnivores

 Aquatic Mammals

 Marine Mammals

 Fish

 Intertidal Marine Life

 Reptiles / Amphibians

 Insects

 Wildflowers

**Facilities Symbols:**

 Brochures / Checklists

 Interpretive Displays

 Self-guided Trail

 Guided Tour

 Observation Platform / Viewpoints

 Wheelchair Accessible

 Hiking / Walking Trail

 Picnic / Day Use

 Tent Camping

 Toilets

# Responsible Wildlife Viewing

Public interest in wildlife has never been greater. Birdwatching alone has attracted nearly thirty million North Americans, and every year more than twenty-two percent of Canadians travel to observe and photograph wildlife.

This interest, however, has had its consequences. Although people are more conscious of preserving wildlife, some species have nevertheless experienced frequent harassment by humans, and critical habitats have been damaged by the pressures of increased human visitation.

Modern wildlife viewing demands courtesy and common sense — including respect for animals and their habitats, knowledge of local regulations, and consideration for private property and the activities of others.

Today's ethics for the field include the following:

- Confine your movements to designated trails and roads, wherever provided. This allows animals to adapt to human use in the area and also minimizes your impact on plant life.

- Avoid nesting sites and dens, and respect the resting period of birds and animals. Never touch or feed wild animals. Baby animals are seldom orphaned or abandoned, and it's against the law to take them away.

- Stress is harmful to wildlife, so never chase or flush animals from cover. Use binoculars and keep a respectful distance, for the animal's sake and occasionally for your own.

- Leave the environment, including both the flora and the fauna, unchanged by your visits. Take home only pictures and memories.

- Pets are a hindrance to wildlife viewing. They may chase, injure or kill wild animals, so control your pets or leave them at home.

- Most importantly, we must learn about wildlife: the behaviour and sensitivity of each species. Our knowledge of these animals will help us to be better stewards to wildlife and the areas they inhabit. Confine your movements wherever possible to designated trails, viewing platforms and blinds.

Respect and good judgement by today's wildlife watchers are essential to the preservation of British Columbia's natural heritage for future generations.


Jim Butler

# Photographing Wildlife

The best photographers learn patience. You may need to sit near a pond for hours to gain the trust of beavers, or stand in a marsh all morning for a shot of a heron in flight.

After an extended period of time, many animals and birds will accept you as part of the surrounding territory and resume their normal activities. By moving — slowly — only when the animal is looking the other way, you can often get close enough to mammals such as mule deer and elk for great telephoto shots. Blinds and zoom lenses are helpful, and multi-coloured clothing will help to break up the human form in the animal's eyes.

K. BOWEN

Getting closer than telephoto range to large mammals or even some of the more aggressive birds is hazardous. Although elk look their best during the rutting season in mid-autumn, for example, the bulls can be dangerous at this time. Moose can be aggressive at any time, and shouldn't be approached as closely as other ungulates. Bears should never be approached: use a long lens for them, or use your vehicle as a screen, and remember to compensate for their dark coats by opening up the lens aperture.

Avoid approaching nests too closely: you will not only alarm the birds, but ruin your chances for a stunning photograph. Never attempt to photograph raptors (hawks and owls) while they are laying or incubating eggs as they are very likely to abandon the nest. Stay at a distance, with a tripod and a zoom lens, and wait for the birds to come into your viewing range.

## Framing and Lighting Your Photographs

The early morning hours (until about 10 a.m.), when birds and animals are most active, can be the best times for photography. The early light defines shape and colour better than the intense light of midday, which flattens contrast and washes out colour. Avoid distracting backgrounds in your photographs by focusing as closely as possible on the subject, or by reducing the depth of field. By opening the lens aperture, the background will blur, leaving your subject to stand out in clear focus.

Shoot on the same level as your subject (or slightly below) whenever possible. A photograph taken from above frequently results in the subject's being lost in the background.

Use a faster shutter speed (1/500th of a second or more) for birds in flight, or for running mammals. Also, the use of a motor drive for a rapid succession of shots will increase chances of getting that perfect picture. Panning the camera with a moving animal while clicking the shutter will create an impression of movement, as the background will blur.

Many of the smaller animals and dozens of varieties of birds and wildflowers are seen most often in low-light situations: in deep forest, just after dawn, or near sunset. High-speed film can produce good results under these circumstances.

Flash equipment may provide sharper, more colourful images on dull days, and may help to eliminate distracting shadows, thereby providing better images of dark-coloured birds and small mammals.

Avoid back-lighting, except for special effects. This can work well with flowers.

## Equipment

A **35-mm single lens reflex camera** is most frequently used for wildlife photography, and is all you really need.

Take along an **adequate supply of film**, of varying speeds. It is worthwhile to pack all camera equipment — and film — in waterproof, protective cases. Keep small pouch of silica gel in the case as well to help dry the camera and lenses in high humidity situations.

**Tripods** are a must for low light situations and when slow shutter speeds are to be used. To obtain high quality, sharply focused photographs, the camera must be perfectly still and this can only be achieved with a tripod. Lenses larger than 300 mm usually require a tripod or other support for the camera.

Appropriate **lenses** and **filters** can improve your photographs. A telephoto lens that can focus down to about 15 feet is almost essential for birds and mammals. Extension tubes can reduce the focus distance even further, thus increasing the image size on the film.

A lens that will focus to nine inches will be needed for recording wildflowers and butterflies. Zoom lenses are particularly convenient, but will reduce the amount of incoming light, which may present problems.

A polarizing filter will cut reflection, intensify colour and help in photographing fish in streams.

While portable **blinds** are ideal for all wildlife photography, excellent pictures can be obtained from the windows of a parked car, a canoe, or anything else that helps to hide or break up the human shape in the eyes of mammals and birds. Even a piece of burlap draped over the head and upper body can help.

Take along a **notebook** with a waterproof cover and a pencil (which writes more easily than pen on damp paper). In it, you can record the time and location of your shots to assist in organizing your photographs after the trip. You may also find it useful to record lens aperture settings, lenses used, film speed, and so on, in order to more quickly build your wildlife photography expertise.

*Great blue heron*

# Ecoprovinces of British Columbia

### Georgia Depression

This broad sheltered basin harbours the Strait of Georgia, the adjacent lowlands and the Gulf Islands. An effective rainshadow appears in the lee  of the Vancouver Island Range while more precipitation falls on the Lower Mainland side. Overall, however, this area experiences the highest number of days of sunshine in the province. A variety of rich habitats includes Douglas-fir, arbutus and red-alder forests, agricultural lands and large estuaries. The flat lowlands and moderate climate attract a diversity of wildlife and the highest numbers of people in the province.

### Coast & Mountains

This is the western edge of the province and consists of the Coastal Mountains, islands and the Continental Shelf. The major climatic process is determined by the arrival of frontal systems carrying moist air off the Pacific Ocean, causing high rainfall as these systems are lifted by the mountains. The land-  scape includes wave-beaten shorelines, coastal plains and rugged ice-capped mountains cut by wide rivers, fiords and estuaries. Vegetation consists primarily of large temperate rainforests with alpine tundra on the mountain summits.

### Southern Interior

 This is the southern-most portion of the interior plateau system. Its landscape lies in the rainshadow of the Coast and Cascade mountains, which combined with the intrusion of warm air from the Great Basin to the south, creates some of the warmest and driest areas in the province. Higher eleva-tions receive regular rain and snowfall in the winter, but this is the mildest area in the interior. Habitats include dry grasslands in the major valleys, ponderosa-pine and Douglas-fir forests, large deep lakes and numerous small wetlands and rivers.

### Central Interior

The extensive plateau system in the centre of the province includes the Chilcotin, Cariboo and Nechako plateaus. While the area lies in the rainshadow of the Coastal Mountains, it is still influenced by the moderating flow of Pacific air. It is a climate of cold winters and warm summers. Seven vegetation zones occur here,  ranging from dry sagebrush grasslands in the deep Fraser River Badlands to dense lodgepole pine forests across most of the plateau's uplands. Wetlands and small lakes are numerous.

### Southern Interior Mountains

The vast mountain ranges of the southeastern part of the province include the Columbian Mountains, the Continental Ranges of the Rocky Mountains and the Rocky Mountain Trench. The western slopes of the mountains draw more precipitation, and snowfall is heavy during winter. The trench is warm and clear in the summer but serves as an access route for outbreaks of cold arctic air. Dense conifer forests are common here, though dry forests occupy the southern valleys, and alpine tundra and barren rock etch the mountain summits.

### Sub-boreal Interior

Located in the north-central portion of the province, this landscape includes broad level plateaus bordered by the Skeena, Omineca and Rocky mountains. Though the mountains are typically wet, much of this area is in the rain-shadow of the Coastal Mountains. While the summers are warm, in winter the Arctic front frequently descends to the southern edge of this region. Vegetation is primarily dense conifer forests of spruce, pine and fir, with scattered wetlands and deciduous forests. Alpine Tundra occurs on the mountain summits.

### Northern Boreal Mountains

The extensive mountains and plateaus in the far north-central part of the province are separated by wide valleys and lowlands. The high mountain ranges to the west create a rain-shadow causing some areas of the region to be very dry. Precipitation is evenly distributed through the mild summers and long cold winters.
Much of the habitat is high lodgepole pine or spruce forests and rolling alpine tundra though the lower elevations have extensive willow scrub and wetlands.

### Boreal & Taiga Plains

These two ecoprovinces consist of the extensive level plateaus and lowlands in the northeastern portion of the province. Cold Arctic air is unimpeded from the north and may easily blanket the area through winter and spring. Summers are warm and dry except for occasional rains. The  plateaus, plains and prairies of the Boreal Plains contain aspen parkland, spruce forests and some sub-alpine fir in the western reaches. The more northerly Taiga Plains represent a flat lowland of muskeg and black- and white-spruce forests. Wetlands and small lakes are common in both areas.

PHOTOS ON PAGES 12 & 13 BY D.A. DEMARCHI

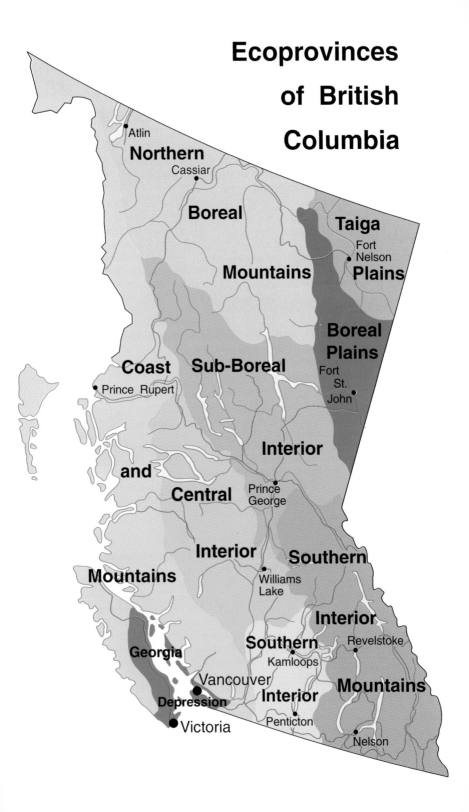

# Ecoprovinces of British Columbia

Atlin

**Northern**

Cassiar

**Boreal**

**Taiga**

Fort Nelson

**Mountains**

**Plains**

**Boreal Plains**

**Coast**

**Sub-Boreal**

Prince Rupert

Fort St. John

**Interior**

**and**

**Central**

Prince George

**Interior**

**Southern**

Mountains

Williams Lake

**Interior**

Revelstoke

**Southern**

**Mountains**

Kamloops

**Georgia**

Vancouver

**Interior**

**Depression**

Victoria

Penticton

Nelson

# GEORGIA DEPRESSION

The sheltered Gulf Islands and the coastal lowlands that cradle the Strait of Georgia may have wet winters but the warm, sunny summers have the clearest skies of any area of the province. The rich and varied habitats of this area support the highest diversity of birds in B.C.

The mild climate and significant size of the wetlands of the Fraser River Delta make it a critical stopover and wintering area for migratory waterfowl, raptors and songbirds. Large numbers of waterbirds also winter in the bays and surge narrows along the coast. Rivers teem with salmon in the fall and early winter. Wildlife such as black-tailed deer and coyote are abundant in the lowlands while Roosevelt elk and cougar are found in more remote areas.

Porpoise, seals, sea lions and killer whales are frequently seen throughout the Strait of Georgia.

Black numbers refer to the page numbers of wildlife viewing sites.

# Active Pass / Bellhouse Provincial Park

The narrow pass between Galiano and Mayne islands is an area of turbulent tides and swirling currents. Constant upswelling creates a productive marine environment which attracts herring, salmon, marine mammals and a wide variety of bird life. Cormorants congregate on rocky islands and cliffs throughout the pass and thousands of Pacific loons migrate through the area in spring. Bald eagles are commonly seen roosting in snags along the island shorelines.

An ideal way to view the wildlife here is from the ferry which travels between Tsawwassen and Swartz Bay. For a longer visit, head ashore on Galiano Island and drive to Bellhouse Provincial Park. The park provides a peaceful setting for a picnic among porpoise, harbour seals and pelagic birds. Pods of killer whales can occasionally be spotted. Sea lions, which are often seen at Helen's Point on Mayne Island or Collinson Reef on Galiano, are most abundant between July and October when Chinook and Coho salmon are running.

*The pelagic cormorant is the smallest of the three cormorant species found on the B.C. coast.*

*Thousands of Pacific loons gather at Active Pass during spring migration.*

**Directions:** Take ferry between Tsawwassen and Swartz Bay. Galiano Island: take Sturdies Bay Road, left on Burrel Rd. and left on Jack Dr. to Bellhouse Provincial Park.

Ministry of Parks,
Victoria 387-4363
Dept. of Fisheries and Oceans,
Duncan 746-6221

# Sidney Spit Provincial Marine Park

Located four kilometres offshore, Sidney Island harbours a sheltered lagoon, a large sandspit and one of the largest salt marshes on the B.C. coast. Black brants, oldsquaws and a variety of other waterfowl forage in the lush salt marsh. During spring and fall, black-bellied plovers, oystercatchers and a host of other shorebirds descend on the spit in great numbers. Great blue herons roost high in the trees at the southeast end of the lagoon in the spring and early summer. Marbled murrelets, pigeon guillemots, harbour seals and river otters are frequently seen swimming offshore.

While walking through the red alder, Douglas fir and arbutus forests, watch for screech owls, rabbits, garter snakes and squirrels. Deer are common throughout the park. In the summer, little brown bats can be seen hanging under the eaves of cook shelters and other buildings.

*Both parents of the black oystercatcher share in the incubation of their young.*

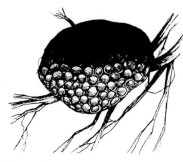

*Wasp nest*

**Directions:** Take the foot passenger ferry or your own boat from Sidney to the government wharf in the lagoon.

Ministry of Parks,
Victoria 387-4363

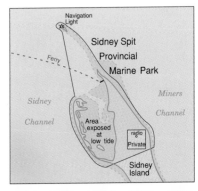

# Goldstream Provincial Park

M. NAGA

CANADIAN WILDLIFE SERVICE

*The moist coastal forests support a multitude of banana slugs which reach up to 15 cm in length.*

This area is characterized by peaceful trails winding through old growth forest, wildflowers, waterfalls and a clear, meandering river which flows into a salt marsh at Finlayson Arm. Though only sixteen kilometres from Victoria, it harbours a variety of bird life, including Barrow's goldeneye, bufflehead and other waterfowl attracted to the winter marsh.

Summer is best for viewing migratory songbirds, including willow flycatchers, common nighthawks and Swainson's thrushes. Year round birds include downy woodpeckers, red-breasted nuthatches, great blue herons and red-tailed hawks.

Between October and December thousands of salmon spawn in the Goldstream River. This attracts gulls and eagles, which scavenge salmon carcasses, and American dippers, which feed on salmon eggs. On cool, damp days in the spring and fall you'll see red-backed salamanders and rough-skinned newts on the forest floor, and you even glimpse a black-tailed deer. The visitors' centre will provide directions to the best viewing sites.

**Directions:** Drive 16 km north of Victoria on the Island Highway. The park is at the south of Finlayson Arm.

Ministry of Parks,
Victoria 387-4363

# Swan Lake Nature Sanctuary

This alluring lake and the surrounding thirty-six hectares of upland habitat offer a beautiful setting for viewing wildlife close to Victoria. Several ponds and oak-forested rocky outcrops provide a range of habitats for wildlife and wildflowers. Every year, seasonal flooding greatly expands the lake area, and consequently attracts migrating waterfowl in large numbers. A variety of water birds, including great blue herons and pied-billed grebes reside here. Red-tailed hawks are common visitors. Downy woodpeckers and many other forest birds inhabit the oak forests and upland scrub habitat. In spring and summer, little brown bats forage in the area. Muskrats and river otters can be seen throughout the year.

A 2.5 km trail, which includes 250 m of floating boardwalk, floating wharves and bird blinds, provides excellent opportunities for viewing wildlife. The nature house, complete with exhibit area, native plant garden and library will enhance your visit to this sanctuary.

PROVINCE OF BRITISH COLUMBIA

*The downy woodpecker is B.C.'s smallest and closely resembles the larger hairy woodpecker.*

**Directions:** From Victoria Centre: North on Blanshard, right on McKenzie, right on Rainbow, left on Ralph and right on Swan Lake Road to park entrance.

Swan Lake Christmas Hill Nature Sanctuary
479-0211

# Somenos Marsh

This rich wetland ecosystem is teeming with food, and supports a multitude of waterfowl during spring and fall migrations. Many species of waterfowl, including Canada geese, mallards and widgeons spend their winters here. Willow shrubs and the seasonally wet meadows are frequented by songbirds such as marsh wrens, warblers and yellowthroats, which are particularly common. The area also provides feeding grounds for ospreys, northern harriers, red-tailed hawks and merlins.

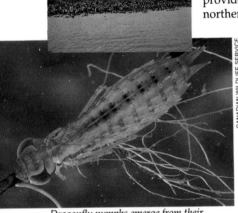

Wooded areas at the north end of the lake provide habitats for a variety of owls and other forest birds. Green-backed herons and short-eared owls have also been sighted here. Great blue herons are plentiful, especially in winter and spring. The lake area is also the home of Pacific treefrogs, garter snakes, toads, muskrats and beavers. Invertebrate life includes numerous aquatic insects, dragonflies and various butterflies.

*Dragonfly nymphs emerge from their aquatic environment in early summer to hatch into the adult stage of their life cycle.*

*Beaver cuttings*

**Directions:** Drive 1 km north of Duncan on Highway 1. Turn east into parking lot along highway.

Ministry of Environment,
Nanaimo 758-3951

*GEORGIA DEPRESSION*

# Courtenay River Estuary

*The Pacific dogwood is an attractive native tree that thrives in moist soils in the understory of coniferous forests.*

*The saw-whet owl, only 18 cm tall, nests in abandoned woodpecker holes. They are, primarily, nocturnal hunters.*

*In winter, trumpeter swans are often seen in upland fields and pastures where they graze on fresh grass, often to the farmers' annoyance.*

This fertile estuarine environment is internationally recognized as a crucial staging area for the waterfowl and shorebirds which migrate up and down the B.C. coast. The estuary also provides nesting and overwintering habitats for thousands of other birds. Up to 2,000 trumpeter swans, representing a significant portion of the world's trumpeter swan population, winter in and around the estuary and are commonly seen feeding in the fields near Courtenay and Comox, where large flocks of western grebes congregate during their spring and fall migrations.

In the spring, the grebes are joined by seals, osprey, eagles, loons, gulls, and various marine birds to feast on large schools of spawning herring. Black brants also stop here in spring to feed on eel grass, their favourite food. Look for large groups of scoters during the summer months, and in the fall scan the estuary for large numbers of black-bellied plovers, western sandpipers and other migrating shorebirds.

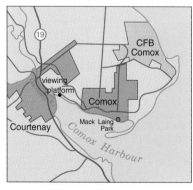

**Viewing Access Points:** Mack Laing Park, the viewing platform at the mouth of the river, or Marine Drive on the south shore.

Ministry of Environment,
Nanaimo 758-3951

# Nanaimo Harbour

Each year, between December and March, vast schools of herring gather in Nanaimo Harbour to spawn. This consequently attracts large numbers of seals, sea lions and birds which feed on the herring. At Harmac, sea lions often rest on log booms near the pulp mill. Gulls and bald eagles roost in the trees and along the rocky shorelines. The sandstone cliffs along Gabriola Island are used by gulls and other nesting marine birds which inhabit the harbour. Cormorants are particularly abundant.

A. GRASS

*Hundreds of Steller's sea lions, which can weigh up to 1000 kg, gather here each winter.*

During the winter months, grebes, great blue herons, scoters and goldeneyes congregate in the Nanaimo River Estuary. Various waterfowl such as geese and trumpeter swans are particularly numerous in spring and fall. Boating through the harbour is the best way to see wildlife. Charters and boat launches are available at many of the marinas in the Nanaimo area.

*Surf scoter*

**Directions:** Drive 5 km south of the ferry terminal at Departure Bay. Parking is available at several locations along the west side of the harbour.

Ministry of Environment, Nanaimo 758-3951

*GEORGIA DEPRESSION*

# Stamp Falls Provincial Park

The Stamp River flows through forests of red cedar and Douglas fir, and is one of the best sites on Vancouver Island to see spawning salmon. The main attraction at Stamp Falls is the run of 100,000 to 300,000 sockeye that fight their way through the rapids of the Stamp and Somas rivers to spawn in Great Central Lake. Up to 80,000 chinook and 60,000 coho also spawn here. River trails and a fish ladder provide excellent viewing opportunities. Pacific lamprey occur on the downstream side of the ladder.

American dippers, harlequin ducks, buffleheads and belted kingfishers can be observed along the river. During salmon runs glaucous-winged gulls are especially abundant. Red squirrels are common from May to October, and black-tailed deer wander through the area year round.

The Robertson Creek Hatchery, 3 km downstream from Great Central Lake, is a good place to see salmon in a rearing facility.

*A female sockeye will carry up to 4,000 eggs which she lays in several nests, called redds, in the gravel of the stream bed.*

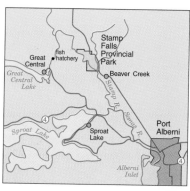

**Directions:** Drive 20 km north from Port Alberni along Beaver Creek Road to the park entrance.

Ministry of Parks,
Parksville 248-3931

*GEORGIA DEPRESSION*

# Parksville / Qualicum

B.C. PARKS

The Parksville/Qualicum area hosts an extraordinary abundance and diversity of birds. More than 225 species of birds visit or reside in the area, but it is most famous for the 20,000 black brant geese that stop here from March to May while on migration. The annual brant festival, which is held in the middle of April, is well worth attending.

Habitats range from estuarine marsh and tidal flats to second growth Douglas fir forests and upland meadows. There are four main viewing sites in the area. Parksville Bay and the Englishman River Estuary provide opportunities to view seabirds and raptors through-

*Black brants stop along the B.C. coast during spring migration to feed on eelgrass.*

out the year. Between November and December eagles are also attracted to the salmon runs here.

Nanoose Harbour, a National Wildlife Area, supports a variety of wintering waterbirds, including trumpeter swans. At the Little Qualicum River Estuary you can see herons, wintering waterbirds and marine mammals during the herring spawn in the spring. Hamilton Swamp is home to deer, elk, bear, beaver and leopard frogs.

**Directions:** Drive 25 km north of Nanaimo. Stop along the coast between Nanoose Bay and Bowser.

Ministry of Environment, Nanaimo 758-3951
Canadian Wildlife Service, Qualicum Beach 752-9611

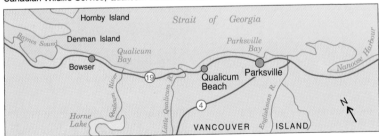

*GEORGIA DEPRESSION*

24

# Strathcona Provincial Park

This park, the oldest in B.C. and the largest on Vancouver Island, encompasses montane slopes, rugged wilderness mountains, lakes and clear flowing rivers. Majestic mountain scenes surround the visitor here, and a walk through old growth forests introduces a host of unique plants and animals.

In winter, trumpeter swans can be found at Buttle Lake and Roosevelt elk may be seen grazing in woodlands along the Elk River at the north end of the park. In spring, the elk move to higher elevations. At the south end of Buttle Lake near Thelwood Creek, a beaver pond and a flood plain are the homes of beavers, black bears and black-tailed deer. Spring and early summer are the best times to see these animals. Paradise meadows, just west of the Mount Washington ski area, produce spectacular shows of wildflowers in the summer. Steller's jays, gray jays, rufous hummingbirds and both blue and ruffled grouse are also abundant.

*The bull Roosevelt elk, which can weigh up to 500 kg, will bugle during rutting as a challenge to other bulls and as an expression of dominance over a herd of females.*

**Directions:** For Elk River and Buttle Lake, travel 40 km west from Campbell River on Highway 28. For Paradise Meadows, travel west from Courtenay and follow the signs to the park.

Ministry of Parks,
Parksville 248-3931

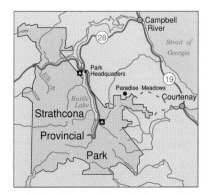

# Mitlenatch Island Provincial Park

This island harbours the largest seabird nesting colony in the Strait of Georgia.* Sizeable colonies of glaucous-winged gulls, pelagic cormorants and pigeon guillemots make the island a very intriguing stop. Rhinoceros auklets can be seen swimming below nesting colonies of cormorants. In spring and fall, flocks of migrating shorebirds feed along the beaches. More than two hundred harlequin ducks spend the summer along the shoreline near Camp Bay. Summer is also a good time for viewing barn swallows, tree swallows and bald eagles.

Marine life, including oysters, crabs, urchins, chitons and colourful starfish are plentiful in the intertidal zone. Seals are quite common and Steller's sea lions sometimes loaf on the rocks at the base of West Hill. Open meadows display a variety of colourful wildflowers from early spring through late summer. Wandering garter snakes, which can reach up to a metre in length, live on the island and can be seen around the gull colonies in spring and early summer.

*Between May 15 and July 31, park visitors must remain on trails to avoid nesting seabirds.*

*Starfish have an internal hydraulic system which operates hundreds of tiny tube feet which they use for feeding and for clinging to rocks.*

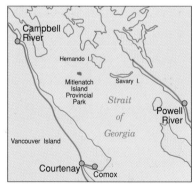

**Directions:** Access by water, 19 km from Campbell River. Charters available. Boat tie ups at Camp Bay or anchor at Northwest Bay.

Ministry of Parks,
Parksville 248-3931

# Iona Beach Regional Park

Located at the mouth of the Fraser River's northern arm, this park contains sandy beaches, lagoons, lush river marsh and open fields. Iona Island boasts the highest annual Christmas bird count in the country, and several rare birds have been seen here. Songbirds abound and shorebirds, especially sandpipers, can be found in vast numbers on the extensive sand flats which are exposed at low tide.

Throughout the marshes many species of waterfowl can be seen, including blue herons, loons, grebes, green-winged teals and pintails. Watch for short-eared owls and other raptors as they glide over the open fields in search of mice. A visitor can walk through grassy fields along the windswept shoreline, or can stroll down the 3.5 km walking trail that stretches into the Strait of Georgia in a narrow jetty. This trail is a good place for viewing seals and a variety of bird life.

*Great blue herons stand motionless for long periods as they wait for prey to move within striking distance of their spear-like bill.*

**Directions:** Drive towards Vancouver International Airport on Sea Island. Follow signs to Iona Island.

Ministry of Environment,
Surrey 584-8822
G.V.R.D. Regional Parks,
Burnaby 432-6350

*GEORGIA DEPRESSION*

# Reifel Migratory Bird Sanctuary

*Tens of thousands of snow geese descend on Reifel Sanctuary each fall. They come from breeding grounds as far away as Wrangell Island in the U.S.S.R.*

*The wood duck is a cavity nesting bird frequently found along waterways associated with dense stands of trees or shrubs in south-central B.C.*

This estuarine marsh, located at the mouth of the Fraser River, supports Canada's largest wintering population of waterfowl. Freshwater ponds, forests, open fields and salt marshes attract more than 230 species of birds. During spring and fall migrations, vast numbers of birds visit the sanctuary. The chorus of tundra and trumpeter swans and several species of geese creates an exciting atmosphere throughout the site, which is particularly famous for the large flocks of of up to 40,000 snow geese. In October the annual snow goose festival attracts hundreds of keen birders.

The area also supports great blue herons, hawks and owls. Songbirds, including goldfinches and kinglets, nest throughout the forest and shrub areas, while the extensive mudflats attract thousands of shorebirds. Numerous birds also nest here, and broods of ducklings and goslings are a common sight in May and June. An extensive system of trails and a viewing tower provide outstanding opportunities for bird watching.

**Directions:** Drive 20 km south of Vancouver on Highway 99 to Ladner. Follow the Reifel Migratory Bird Sanctuary signs to Westham Island.

Ministry of Environment,
Surrey 584-8822
B.C. Waterfowl Society,
Delta 946-6980

*GEORGIA DEPRESSION*

# Boundary Bay

Boundary Bay is amongst the greatest bird-watching habitats in Canada and a critical stopover on the Pacific Flyway for birds moving to and from breeding grounds in Canada, Alaska and the U.S.S.R. Its estuarine marsh habitat is one of the largest on the Pacific Coast, incorporating salt marshes, eel grass beds and mud flats. The adjoining uplands include old pasture, natural grassland and agricultural field

*Short-eared owls can be found in Boundary Bay in record numbers.*

habitats, which support an abundance of voles and mice, and consequently attract Canada's highest density of wintering raptors. Northern harriers, red-tailed and rough-legged hawks are common.

Hundreds of thousands of western sandpipers and other shorebirds feed on the mud flats in spring and fall as do flocks of black brants and other waterfowl visiting the area during their migrations. Tens of thousands of ducks, geese, shorebirds and other waterbirds overwinter here, and thousands of gulls make daily flights between the bay and the surrounding fields. Seals can often be seen on the mud flats near the Serpentine and Nicomekl rivers in Mud Bay, where a variety of invertebrate life is revealed at low tide. The best way to view this area is by walking the dykes which run along the shoreline.

*Crane fly*

**Directions:** From Highway 10 turn south on 64th, 72nd or 112th St. to the dyke. Blackie Spit and 12th Ave. also provide access to the site.

Ministry of Environment,
Surrey 584-8822
G.V.R.D. Parks,
Vancouver 432-6350

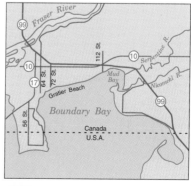

# Serpentine Wildlife Area

This wildlife area consists of 72 hectares of wetland surrounded by 40 hectares of dry meadows and agricultural land devoted to feed crops for waterfowl. The site provides a freshwater sanctuary for birds which inhabit the nearby salt marshes of Boundary Bay. Several species of waterfowl congregate here during winter and spring. Some, like Canada geese, stay on one of the many small islands to nest and raise their young.

Watch for ring-necked pheasants, which often flush as you walk around the marsh. Shorebirds and a variety of raptors, including northern harriers, are frequently seen here. Red-winged blackbirds, house finches and song sparrows are a few of the many species of songbirds common to the area. The marsh is surrounded by a system of trails, and overlooked by two elevated platforms which are excellent for viewing wildlife.

*The female Canada goose incubates her 4-6 eggs for 25-28 days. The first broods are usually seen at the Serpentine Wildlife Area in late April.*

*Shooting star*

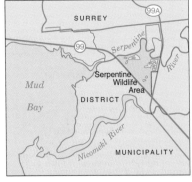

**Directions:** Drive 40 km south of Vancouver on Highway 99. Turn north on King George Highway to the Serpentine River bridge.

Ministry of Environment,
Surrey 584-8822
Ducks Unlimited,
Surrey 591-1104

*GEORGIA DEPRESSION*

# Burnaby Lake Regional Park

An oasis in the heart of the city, Burnaby Lake offers a quiet sanctuary for both people and wildlife. This marshy lake, which is bordered by lush coniferous and deciduous forests, yields a diversity of habitats that support songbirds, waterfowl, birds of prey and aquatic mammals. Here you can paddle a canoe or kayak along the calm waters which are decorated with yellow iris and pond lily and listen to the magical sounds of the marsh.

Nesting boxes for wood ducks can be found throughout this area, and provide good opportunities for viewing these birds. Many ducks and geese nest in the area, and their young broods are commonly seen in the summer.

In early September, migrating shore-birds are a frequent sight. Listen for great horned owls while walking along one of the many forest trails, and at dusk watch for little brown bats and common nighthawks as they feed on airborne insects.

*Northern harriers feed almost exclusively on rodents and are often seen flying just a few feet off the ground. Males are grey, females are white and young are brown.*

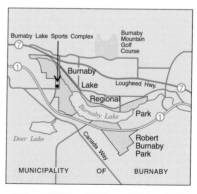

*Pond lily*

The Burnaby Lake nature house is open from 9 a.m. to 5 p.m. from May through September.

**Directions:** 20 km east of downtown Vancouver, take the Kensington or Cariboo exit north off Highway 1. Access nature house on Piper Ave. south off Winston St.

Ministry of Environment,
Surrey 584-8822
G.V.R.D. Parks,
Burnaby 432-6350

     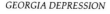

# Pitt-Addington Wildlife Management Area

Bordered by steep coastal mountains, this management area encompasses a system of marsh, tidal lake and river habitats. This site is one of the few areas in the Lower Mainland where you can see sandhill cranes. Three or four pairs of these spectacular birds nest in the Pitt Marsh each spring. Otters frolicking along the dykes, or a lone arctic tern winging slowly across the river are some of the other delightful experiences to be found here.

An ecological reserve at the site supports a host of birds as well as unique plants, such as sundew. A trail through the reserve leads to a viewpoint overlooking a marsh, where deer and black bear are often seen. The area's marsh habitat also provides breeding and wintering grounds for many species of waterfowl and shorebirds. Up to 200 trumpeter swans winter here. In spring, ospreys nest on river pilings and are frequently seen hovering over the river.

B.C. PARKS

PROVINCE OF BRITISH COLUMBIA

*The sundew is a unique marsh plant that secretes a sticky substance on tiny plant hairs to catch insects for food.* (top)

Look for white water lilies which bloom in the Katzie Marsh in early spring.

**Directions:** Drive east of Port Coquitlam on Loughheed Highway to the Pitt River. Turn north on Coast Meridian Dr. to Minnekhada Regional Park or follow the signs to Pitt Lake.

Ministry of Environment, Surrey 584-8822

*GEORGIA DEPRESSION*

# Harrison River / Kilby Provincial Park

The Harrison River, which meanders through the flat lowlands of the Fraser Valley, creates extensive sand and mud flats and provides loafing and feeding areas for a multitude of waterfowl, shorebirds and other water birds. Spring is best for birdwatching, but in the winter several waterfowl species, such as the trumpeter swan, can still be seen at Harrison Bay and along the Harrison River. The large cottonwood trees that line the riverbanks are common perches for hundreds of bald eagles, which gather here between November and February to feed on the five species of salmon that spawn here annually. Look for salmon in creeks and side channels. Woodland and brushy areas along the lower Chehalis River offer habitats for songbirds and food for the beavers that build lodges and dams along the river.

*Immature bald eagles are brown in colour. They develop their contrasting black body and white tail and head after their fourth or fifth year.*

Interesting sites nearby include the Chehalis River hatchery and the Weaver Creek spawning channels. Both are located along the Morris Valley Road on the west side of the Harrison River.

**Directions**: Drive 25 km east of Agassiz or 25 km west of Dewdney on Highway 7 to the Harrison River. Just south of the Harrison River bridge, turn south and follow signs to Kilby Provincial Park.

Ministry of Environment, Surrey 584-8822
Ministry of Parks, Sardis 858-7161

# COAST & MOUNTAINS

Persistent winds and rain lash this coastal area of islands, fiords and rugged ice-capped mountains. The lush temperate rainforests are draped in mosses and ferns. Western hemlock trees grow from sea level to the subalpine and form some of the grandest of all conifer forests in the country. Western red cedar are common in the lowlands while yellow cedar and mountain hemlock grow at higher elevations. The coastline is broken by rocky and sandy beaches and by the rich habitats of the Pacific estuaries. Salmon streams, an important part of the coastal geography, support a great diversity of life here.

Marine mammals such as gray and killer whales, sea lions and harbour seals live throughout the coast and some of the largest seabird nesting colonies in North America are found here. Black-tailed deer, black bear and a host of other mammals live throughout the region. On the mainland, grizzly bears are common and the rugged bluffs of the high elevation forests are frequently inhabited by mountain goats.

Northern

Coastal

Mountains

Nass

Basin

(37)

Queen
Charlotte
Lowland

Prince
Rupert

Terrace (16)

Nass
Ranges

(42)

(41)

Queen
Charlotte
Ranges

Coastal
Gap

Bella
Coola

Pacific
and
Cascade
Ranges

Continental
Shelf

(38)

Western

(19)

(99)

(1)

Vancouver

(39)

(40)

Black numbers refer
to the page numbers
of wildlife viewing sites.

Island

(36)

Vancouver

(35)

Victoria

# French Beach Provincial Park

Against a backdrop of breathtakingly scenic views across the Strait of Juan de Fuca, this park contains a golden stretch of beach, lush coastal forest and several clear-flowing creeks, making it an ideal place to watch for whales migrating along the coast. Gray and humpback whales pass by here on their way to and from their northern feeding grounds. Late March to early May, and late August to October are the best times to look for these impressive animals. The whales can be located by the spouts of water they blow high into the air when they surface. They usually show only a glimpse of themselves, but occasionally their giant tail flukes break the water, or they thrust their massive bodies into the air, crashing down with a huge splash.

The park is also a good place to watch seabirds, waterfowl and shorebirds. Eagles and osprey can often be seen circling overhead. Just offshore, seals and sea lions cruise the shoreline in search of food.

D. CULVER

B.C. PARKS

*In order to grow, red rock crabs, as with other arthropods, shed their hard shell exoskeleton and grow a new one.*

*Using deep sound channels in the ocean, humpback whales can communicate with each other through their songs across thousands of miles of water.*

One feeding technique of the humpback whale is to concentrate small schools of fish by encircling them in a wall of air bubbles, blown from their blowholes.

**Directions:** Drive 20 km west of Sooke on Highway 14.

Ministry of Parks,
Victoria 387-4363

# Pacific Rim National Park

*Long Beach is a spectacular beach that stretches for 25 km just south of Tofino.*

*The tufted puffin nests on cliffs along the B.C. and Alaska coasts.*

This untamed park, which stretches for 40 km along Vancouver Island's west coast, contains old growth forests, spectacular sandy beaches and many kilometres of rocky shoreline. Intertidal areas display magnificent marine life, such as giant barnacles, mussels and starfish. The beaches and tidal flats provide habitats for numerous birds. Many species of waterfowl, shorebirds and seabirds winter along the coast between November and March, and large flocks of birds migrate through the area in spring. Walks along the beaches and trips along the coast by boat or kayak offer the best opportunities for birdwatching.

Whale-watching is an added attraction of this park. Gray and humpback whales migrate along the coast throughout the months of March, April, October and November. Some gray whales take up residence here in the summer. Steller's sea lions and seals are frequently seen on the rocky shorelines. Mink, otters and raccoons are common throughout the park. Watch for bears, deer and a variety of songbirds along the forest trails.

*Starfish (facing page)*

A. THYSSE

**Directions:** Drive west from Parksville on Highway 4 to Tofino or Ucluelet. Access the south park area from Bamfield.

Parks Canada Visitor Information, Tofino 726-4212
Parks Canada Interpretive Centre, Ucluelet 726-7333

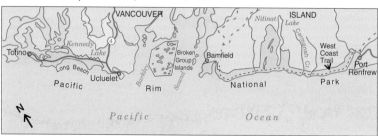

*COAST & MOUNTAINS*

# Blackfish Sound / Johnstone Strait

Located in the northern reaches of Johnstone Strait, Blackfish Sound provides unique opportunities for sighting killer whales, dall porpoises and harbour seals. Dall porpoises may be seen breaking the surface of open water while seals commonly gather around the kelp beds and rocky shorelines. Between June and October pods of killer whales, usually led by a large male, travel these waters in search of food. Whales are often seen at rubbing beaches in the ecological reserve at the Tsitika River estuary. IMPORTANT: Boaters are asked to refrain from entering the reserve and to view whales elsewhere because of the sensitivity of the site.

*Killer whales, which weigh up to 5.4 tonnes, feed on fish, seals, sea lions, and porpoise. They travel in close family units called pods.*

Bald eagles can be found perching on snags along the shorelines. The numerous islands provide nesting and roosting habitats for seabirds such as pigeon guillemots, murrelets, cormorants and a variety of gulls.

Marinas, camping grounds, and most service facilities are available at Telegraph Cove and Port McNeill.

*Double-crested cormorants often nest on rocky cliffs where both parents incubate the eggs and care for the young.*

**Directions:** Take a boat east from Telegraph Cove or Alert Bay, or north of Sayward. The sound is located 30 km east of Port McNeill.

Ministry of Environment,
Nanaimo 758-3951
Federal Fisheries Department,
Vancouver 754-0235

# Coquihalla Canyon Provincial Park

The clear waters of the Coquihalla River, which flows through the scenic coastal forests of the Cascade Mountains, provide spawning habitats for fish. At Coquihalla Canyon Provincial Park, the river cuts through a steep canyon. Here, a short walk along the old Kettle Valley railway grade, through four tunnels and across two foot bridges, leads to a viewpoint where you can watch steelhead trout. In July and early August, these large, glistening fish leap dramatically into the air as they struggle against the turbulent rapids. Falling rocks have created narrow chutes along the river, which only these steelhead can jump to spawn upstream.

The mixed forest, which contains cedar, hemlock and Douglas fir, provides habitats for varied thrushes, black-throated gray warblers and many other songbirds. American dippers and tailed frogs are frequently seen along the creek while raccoons, pikas and blacktail deer are common throughout the park.

*Pika are small mammals that do not hibernate. In summer they cut grasses, dry them in the sun and store them in their dens for winter food.*

**Directions:** Drive east of Hope to Kawkawa Lake. Past the lake, take the right fork and turn right at the first crossroads into the park.

Ministry of Environment, Kamloops 374-9717

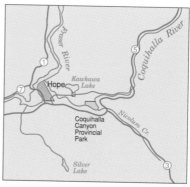

*COAST & MOUNTAINS*

# Manning Provincial Park

Golden-crowned kinglets are tiny birds that spend the winter in Canada when many other birds have migrated south. They feed almost exclusively on insects.

Located high in the Cascade Mountains, this park features extensive trails which provide easy access to clear mountain lakes, dense Engelmann spruce forests and open alpine meadows. In the summer, these meadows are transformed into seas of colour by hectares of wildflowers. The park is an excellent place to view songbirds such as golden-crowned kinglets, red crossbills or Clarke's nutcrackers, which are common, attractive residents.

Columbian and golden-mantled ground squirrels frolic throughout the park and hoary and yellow-bellied marmots are often seen sunning themselves on rocks in the summer. In the strawberry flats area butterflies abound. Several species of dragonfly and other aquatic insects inhabit the lakes, streams and marshes where tailed frogs, harlequin ducks and Barrow's goldeneyes are also found. Visit the interpretive centre 1 km east of the park lodge for detailed information on wildlife viewing sites. Summer is the best time to visit.

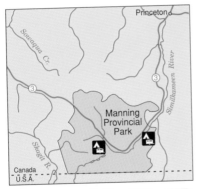

**Directions:** Drive 55 km west of Princeton or 30 km east of Hope on Highway 3 to the park lodge.

Ministry of Parks,
Cultis Lake 858-7161

# Lower Skeena River

*Glaucus-winged gulls breed along the B.C. coast and are distinguished from other large gulls by their light grey, rather than black, wing tips.*

The Skeena cuts its way through rugged coastal mountains to the Pacific Ocean where the river forms a wide, shallow delta dotted with cottonwood- and willow-covered islands. From early March through mid-April, eulachons, sometimes called candlefish, return to the river in great numbers to spawn. This migration attracts seals, sea lions and several species of birds which feed on these small fish. Literally millions of gulls flock to the area. Mew, herring and glaucous-winged gulls are all common. Bald eagles soar overhead while harbour seals and sea lions pull out on sand bars and tidal flats along the river.

During spring and fall, the Skeena is a favourite stop for migrating shorebirds and waterfowl. Bears and moose are sometimes seen along the river and mountain goats frequent south facing slopes along the north side of the highway. The best viewing areas are between the Ecstall and Kasiks rivers on Highway 16. Telegraph Point, 50 km east of Prince Rupert, is a common observation point.

**Directions:** Drive west of Terrace or east of Prince Rupert along the north shore of the Skeena River on Highway 16.

Ministry of Environment, Smithers 847-7303

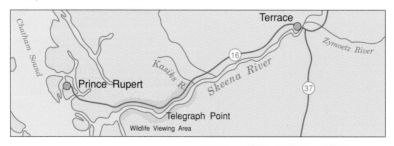

# Delkatla Slough

*Long-billed dowitchers nest in the arctic but stop along the B.C. coast during migration. They are commonly seen in freshwater ponds.*

Delkatla Slough, adjacent to the town of Masset at the north end of the Queen Charlotte Islands, is a diverse marsh ecosystem. Historically, periodic tidal flooding enriched this wetland, creating a significant staging and nesting area for over 100 bird species including sandhill cranes and trumpeter swans. Bald eagles, great blue herons, Canada geese, belted kingfishers, winter wrens and varied thrushes are a few of the common year-round residents which can be found here. The abundant bird life makes this site an exciting viewing area, particularly during spring and fall migrations. Coastal storms also drive large numbers of birds to the slough for protection. This is a good place to look for rare birds which the severe storms occasionally carry off course. Two observation platforms and a network of trails provide good bird watching sites throughout the marsh.

*Winter wren*

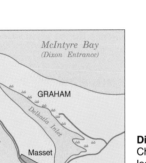

**Directions:** Drive north from Queen Charlotte to Masset. The slough is located on the east shore of Masset Harbour.

Ministry of Environment, Smithers 874-7303

*COAST & MOUNTAINS*

# SOUTHERN INTERIOR

This rolling plateau with deep wide valleys is the hottest and driest area in the province and also has the warmest winters of any interior area. This climate attracts the greatest diversity of birds found in the interior of B.C. Some species, including the ferruginous hawk, prairie falcon, flammulated owl and white-headed woodpecker breed nowhere else in the province. The area also contains the only site in Canada that supports a major wintering population of tundra swan. Pockets of desert in this region boast many unique reptiles. The forests of pine and Douglas fir are inhabited by mule deer and blue grouse while bighorn sheep are found on the rocky grasslands of the region. The clear-flowing rivers, such as the Thompson and Adams, provide excellent spawning grounds for large runs of salmon.

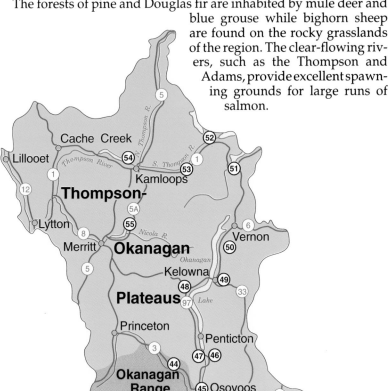

Black numbers refer to the page numbers of wildlife viewing sites.

# Hedley - Keremeos Cliffs

In the early morning and late afternoon, the sun brings out the soft colours of this region's rugged mountain slopes and dry grasslands, and highlights the scenic banks of the Similkameen River. The extensive scree slopes and jagged rock outcrops along the valley's north slopes offer one of the most accessible locations in the province to view mountain goats, especially during spring and fall. Yellow-bellied marmots, chukar partridges and California quail also inhabit these steep mountain slopes while golden eagles are frequently seen soaring overhead. Western rattlesnakes* live in the area, so be careful where you step when hiking. From May to September, watch for mountain bluebirds and many other dryland bird species throughout the valley. Several pull-outs and viewpoints along Highway 3 between Hedley and Keremeos provide good viewing access. Camping and picnic facilities are available in Keremeos.

*The Indian paintbrush flower can be red, yellow, pink or orange and is most common in open moist areas.*

*The only venomous snake in B.C., rattlesnakes occur in the Southern Interior Ecoprovince. They are not generally aggressive, but should not be approached by amateurs. In rattlesnake country, always be careful where you step or put your hands. Poisonous snake bites are serious.

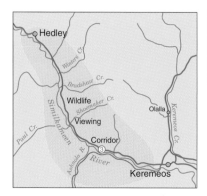

Bighorn sheep are often seen on the Ashnola River Road just south of Highway 3.

**Directions:** Drive along Highway 3 between Hedley and Keremeos. The Ashnola Road is approximately 8 km east of Keremeos.

Ministry of Environment, Penticton 493-8261

# Osoyoos Oxbows

The lush green marsh of the Osoyoos Oxbows provides a striking contrast to the adjacent dry hillsides. The oxbows, which are remnant sections of the meandering Okanagan River, are situated in one of the hottest and driest areas of Canada. The rich riparian marsh complex and surrounding arid habitat create a unique environment which is home to an amazing diversity of species including the western painted turtle, spadefoot toad and canyon wren.

In spring and summer, the marsh is alive with the song of brightly coloured bobolinks, yellow-headed blackbirds and a variety of other songbirds. Great blue herons, waterfowl and shorebirds inhabit the area through the spring, summer and fall as do osprey, which can be seen fishing around the oxbows. The area also supports muskrat, beaver, raccoon, coyote and mule deer. Bats are attracted to the area by the masses of insects which emerge from the oxbows.

*Western painted turtles, the most common turtles in North America, enjoy sunning themselves. Look for them on logs and rocks along the shoreline.*

**Directions:** Drive south of Penticton on Highway 97 and turn east on Road 22. The oxbows lie at the north end of Osoyoos Lake.

Ministry of Environment, Penticton 493-8261

# Vaseux Lake

The dry grasslands of the Vaseux Lake area, which include sagebrush, talus slope and rocky cliff habitats, support a large population of California bighorn sheep. In the fall rutting season, you can watch and hear the large rams charging and butting their great horns together on the hillsides along Highway 97. Bats, fifteen species of which live in the area, are often seen feeding over marshy areas at dusk; this is also a good time to see the beaver which live in the lake and the nearby streams. The marsh, river and lake attract several species of waterfowl which nest in the area and canyon wrens, lazuli buntings and many other songbirds are commonly seen here. Seven species of snake, including the western rattlesnake,* also live in the area. Western painted turtles can frequently be seen basking in the sun in the adjacent oxbows in spring and summer.

*California bighorn sheep adult males have large curling horns and can weigh up to 50 kg more than the females which have short, thin, slightly curved horns.*

*The only venomous snake in B.C., rattlesnakes occur in the Southern Interior Ecoprovince. They are not generally aggressive, but should not be approached by amateurs. In rattlesnake country, always be careful where you step or put your hands. Poisonous snake bites are serious.

**Directions:** Drive 10 km south of Okanagan Falls or 10 km north of Oliver on Highway 97. Follow signs to the provincial park.

Ministry of Environment, Penticton 493-8261
Ministry of Parks, Summerland 494-0321

# Okanagan Falls Provincial Park

Okanagan Falls is a lush oasis in an otherwise arid bunchgrass and sagebrush landscape. The large stands of deciduous trees that grow along the Okanagan River provide habitats for many species of songbirds and other wildlife. The large numbers of insects which emerge here attract swallows, nighthawks and several species of bats. In spring, summer and early fall, bats and nighthawks display impressive aerial manoeuvres as they forage for airborne insects at dusk. In the early evening, nighthawks and high flying big brown bats are the first to arrive while the smaller, lower flying bats join in later, as the evening progresses. Cliff and barn swallows, which are also common here, nest under bridges and feed on insects during the day. The river is also home to beavers, muskrats, garter snakes and several species of waterfowl including gadwalls, common goldeneyes and buffleheads which winter along the river.

*Catching their prey on the wing, common nighthawks feed entirely on insects and are often seen feeding over water.*

*Muskrat*

**Directions:** Drive 1 km south of Highway 97 on Green Lake Road along the west bank of Okanagan River, just west of Okanagan Falls.

Ministry of Environment, Penticton 493-8261
Ministry of Parks, Summerland 494-0321

# Peachland Creek

B.C. PARKS

*Kokanee numbers have dropped drastically in Lake Okanagan over the last few decades. They depend on clear free-flowing creeks, like Peachland, to spawn.*

Peachland Creek, sometimes called Deep Creek, flows through ponderosa pine forests on the west slopes of the Okanagan valley into Okanagan Lake at the town of Peachland. Between mid-September and mid-October, over 5,000 kokanee return here to a 0.5 kilometre stretch of river, one of the few remaining sites on the lake where large numbers of kokanee still spawn. As you walk upstream along the spawning area, the peacefulness of the babbling creek is soon replaced by the thunder of Hadly Falls. When the fish are spawning, American dippers and mallard ducks congregate at the site to feed on fish eggs. Pileated woodpeckers and red squirrels are commonly seen in cottonwood trees along the river. A portion of the river flows through a provincial park which provides picnic and camping sites. A series of trails and bridges throughout the area provide several good kokanee viewing sites.

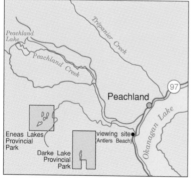

*Mallard ducks are one of the few ducks that actually quack. The female's call sounds like a descending laugh.*

**Directions:** Drive north of Penticton or south of Kelowna on Highway 97 to Peachland. Follow the signs to the provincial park.

Ministry of Environment,
Penticton 493-8261
Ministry of Parks,
Summerland 494-0321

# Mission Creek Regional Park

This unique oasis park, bordered by a growing city, features a clear-flowing creek, with lush marsh and dry ponderosa pine forest benchlands. A network of trails meander through the park, leading to a series of ponds in a woodland of red osier dogwood, alder and cottonwood. Here 100 species of flowering plants, including mountain ladyslippers, pinedrops and spotted coral roots, bloom between April and August. Western painted turtles and muskrat are common in the ponds while squirrel, chipmunk, and other small mammals inhabit upland areas. Little brown bats are frequently seen foraging here around dusk in the summer months.

To the south of Mission Creek, Sutherland Hills Provincial Park offers several trails where swallows, wood ducks, great horned owls and bluebirds can be found. From Mid-September to Mid-October, up to 50,000 kokanee spawn in Mission Creek where a spawning channel provides close up viewing opportunities. White-tailed deer, black bears and coyotes also visit the area in spring and summer.

B.C. PARKS / A. GRASS

*Coral fungi are named for their resemblance to the colorful, hard shells built by colonies of coral polyps.*

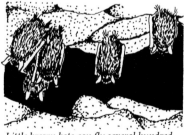

*Little brown bats can fly several hundred miles to caves to hibernate. Hibernation sites in the Okanagan are generally unknown.*

**Directions:** Drive 5 km north of Kelowna on Highway 97. Turn right on Cooper Rd., drive to Springfield Rd. and turn left. Drive north 1 km to parking lot.

Ministry of Environment, Penticton 493-8261
Kelowna Regional District Parks, 861-5224

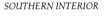

# Kalamalka Lake Provincial Park

*The western rattlesnake is a shy snake that uses poison to stun and kill its prey. With its double-jointed jaw it can swallow food larger than its own head.*

A system of trails winds through virgin grasslands and over rolling hills covered in ponderosa pine. The scenic views of Kalamalka Lake are enhanced by the many species of wildflowers on the grasslands which put on a spectacular show of colour in spring and summer. Western rattlesnakes* are a unique feature here. Many dryland birds, including savannah sparrows and bluebirds, nest here while various other species pass through the area as they migrate north in the spring. Columbian ground squirrels and yellow-bellied marmots are common sights as they scurry through the grasslands and rocky outcrops. Deer, coyotes, badgers and black bears also frequent the site.

*The only venomous snake in B.C., rattlesnakes occur in the Southern Interior Ecoprovince. They are not generally aggressive, but should not be approached by amateurs. In rattlesnake country, always be careful where you step or put your hands. Poisonous snake bites are serious.

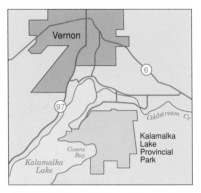

**Directions:** Drive south of Vernon and across the north end of Kalamalka Lake. The park is on the east side of the lake.

Ministry of Environment,
Penticton 493-8261
Ministry of Parks,
Summerland 494-0321

*SOUTHERN INTERIOR*

# Salmon Arm Bay

The tranquil southern bay of Shuswap lake is one of four places in the province where you can see a nesting colony of the elegant western grebe. In early May, the grebes dance across the water in a spectacular exhibition of courtship behaviour. In late June, the young grebes hatch and the birds move to open water where they stay until October, when they migrate to the coast.

The fine sediments which the Salmon River has deposited have created extensive mud flats and lush marshes. Many species of birds are attracted by this habitat. The mudflats provide loafing and feeding areas for waterfowl and a multitude of shorebirds while the cattail marsh is active with red-winged and yellow-headed blackbirds, yellowthroats and sora rails. Osprey, hawks and other raptors frequently soar overhead and painted turtles are common throughout the bay.

*Nesting in colonies, often on floating nests, western grebes lay 3-5 blueish-white eggs which are incubated by both parents.*

The bay is an important rearing ground for young salmon and is the largest river delta on Shuswap Lake.

**Directions:** Turn north off the Trans-Canada Highway in Salmon Arm to Lakeshore Drive. Follow signs to public wharf.

Ministry of Environment, Kamloops 374-9717

# Adams River - Roderick Haig-Brown P. P.*

Every four years, between September and November, over two million crimson-coloured sockeye salmon fight their way up the Fraser and Thompson Rivers to spawn in the Adams River. This is one of the largest congregations of spawning salmon anywhere in the province; the waters appear to turn red. A viewing platform and an extensive system of trails provide excellent opportunities for viewing these fish. In alternate years, smaller numbers of sockeye, spring, coho and pink salmon and rainbow trout spawn in the river.

*Male sockeye salmon fight fiercely with their hooked jaws to ward off other males. Females will fight to protect their nest site.*

The lush forests here provide habitat for small birds and mammals. Warblers frequent the area in spring and summer and ruffed grouse, which can be heard drumming in the spring, often flush as you walk along the trails. Bald eagles, American dippers, mergansers, harlequin ducks and osprey inhabit this river environment. In the evenings and early mornings coyotes, mink and bears are sometimes seen searching for food along the river.

* Provincial Park

**Directions:** Turn north off of Highway 1 at Squilax, just east of Chase. Follow the signs to the park site.

Ministry of Parks,
Kamloops 828-4494

*SOUTHERN INTERIOR*

# South Thompson River

The South Thompson River is kept open year round by the warm waters of Shuswap Lake. Consequently, the area is an important wintering site for over 500 swans and thousands of Canada geese and mallard ducks. In the spring, osprey nest in trees along the river and Canada geese nest in large numbers on small islands dotting the river near Pritchard. Banana Island and Hoffman's Bluff are good places to view the geese with their broods. Spring and fall are the best times to view migrating waterfowl which often stop here to rest. Catbirds, swallows and several species of warbler are common in the willows and wooded areas that border the river. In the summer months, bats frequently fly over the river at dusk.

Watch for pull-outs along the highway where you can stop and scan the river below with your binoculars.

P. GEHLEN

*Tundra swans are large birds that nest in the high arctic and migrate south to winter in freshwater ponds, lakes and rivers.*

California bighorn sheep are seen regularly on the hillsides and bluffs at the east end of Dallas.

**Directions:** Drive along Highway 1 between Kamloops and Chase. There are several viewpoints along the highway.

Ministry of Environment,
Kamloops 374-9717

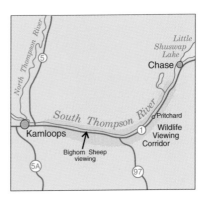

# Tranquille Wildlife Management Area

D. LOW

This area, a flood plain of the Thompson River Valley, experiences yearly flooding which creates a lush environment, an isolated wetland in an otherwise dry sagebrush grassland ecosystem. At peak floodwater the entire area is often under water and during spring migration, over 2,000 Canada geese and many other species of waterfowl, including tundra swan, descend on the flood plains. Great blue herons feed in wetland areas between June and September. In summer and fall, Lewis' woodpeckers and black-billed magpies are common sites in the riparian woodlands. Many species of songbirds gather in the willow thickets during spring and fall migrations.

Mule deer wander through the valley in spring and move onto the surrounding hillsides in the summer; at this time a herd of bighorn sheep can be seen on the hillsides west of Tranquille River. Yellow pine chipmunks and yellow-bellied marmots also inhabit the area, and coyotes are frequently seen hunting in the open meadows.

L. HALVERSON

*Coyotes are very adaptable and will eat almost anything. They are able to maintain populations even in areas of relatively dense human settlement.*

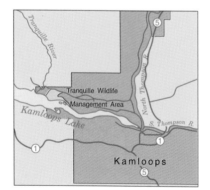

**Directions:** Drive 18 km west of Kamloops city center along the north side of the Thompson River. The site is within the city limits.

Ministry of Environment,
Kamloops 374-9717

# Nicola Valley Corridor

An alternate route to the Coquihalla Highway is the old corridor which runs between Merritt and Kamloops. This scenic road winds past a series of lakes, open grasslands and rolling hills dotted with ponderosa pine and Douglas fir. In April and September, thousands of sandhill cranes pass through the area. Watch for them circling high overhead. Marsh habitats along the lakeshores attracts many species of waterfowl, shorebirds and other water birds. This is one of the best places in the province to view birds of prey such as red-tailed and rough-legged hawk, short eared owl and northern harrier. Kestrels are abundant and can often be seen perching on fenceposts.

The surrounding hills, covered with bunchgrass, support sizable populations of sharp-tailed grouse and provide winter range for mule deer. Watch for coyotes cruising the hillsides or badgers digging for rodents. If you take your time on this trip, you will be rewarded with some memorable experiences.

A. GRASS

*American kestrels are small raptors that feed on grasshoppers, dragonflies and a host of other insects during the summer. In winter they depend on small birds and mice.*

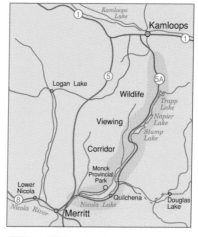

**Directions:** Drive between Merritt and Kamloops on Highway 5A. Pullouts are located along Nicola Lake, Stump Lake, Trapp Lake and Napier Lake.

Ministry of Environment,
Kamloops 374-9717

# CENTRAL INTERIOR

The Fraser River cuts deeply into this broad plateau while rolling uplands rise to mountains in the south and west. Forests of lodgepole pine and trembling aspen dominate the lowlands though Douglas fir is prevalent in the southern portion of this area. Moose are widespread and cougars, black bears, coyotes and wolves are common throughout the region. Mule deer occur in large numbers in the southern plateau while the Fraser River Badlands support several large populations of California bighorn sheep. Small lakes and wetlands that dot the plateau provide excellent habitat for waterfowl and rainbow trout. The world centre for Barrow's goldeneye occurs here as does the only colony of white pelicans in British Columbia.

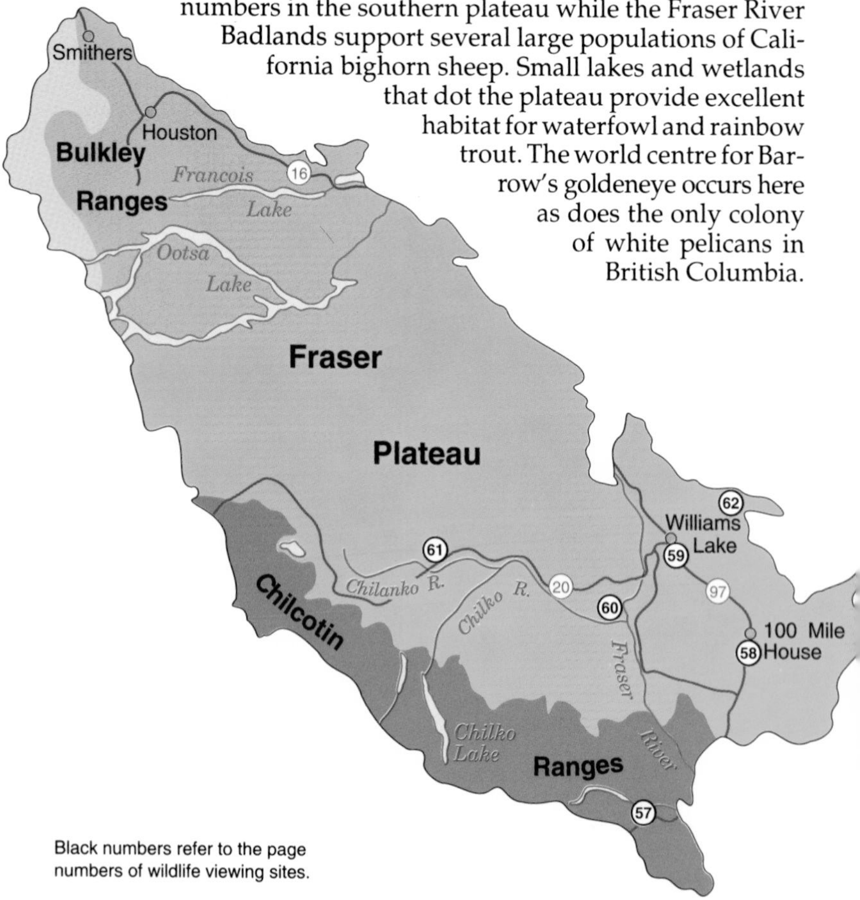

Smithers

Houston

**Bulkley**

*Francois* 16

**Ranges** *Lake*

*Ootsa Lake*

**Fraser**

**Plateau**

62
Williams
59 Lake

61

*Chilanko R.*

*Chilko R.* 20

60

97

100 Mile
58 House

**Chilcotin**

*Chilko Lake*

**Ranges**

*Fraser River*

57

Black numbers refer to the page
numbers of wildlife viewing sites.

# Seton Lake

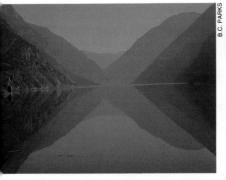

This spectacular landscape of rugged rock bluffs and sparse forests is home to several herds of mountain goats. They can easily be seen roaming the steep hillsides along Seton

*The mountain goat's sharp hooves have a rubbery sole which provides excellent traction on steep and slippery rocks.*

Lake both below and upstream of the Seton Lake Dam. These fascinating animals scramble their way along rocky cliffs to feed on grasses, moss, lichens and conifers. When not feeding, the goats bed down on cliffs and patches of snow or grass. They spend most of their time at higher elevations but move to lowlands in search of other sources of water or mineral licks. They are attracted to south-facing slopes during winter months. In spring, the females give birth to a single kid which stays with the mother for a full year. Cougar and wolves are the goat's primary predators although young are sometimes taken by eagles.

Pika inhabit the lower tallus slopes throughout this landscape. They can be recognized by their distinctive bleat which sounds like a young goat.

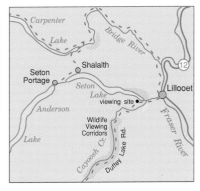

**Directions:** Drive west of Lillooet on Duffey Lake Rd. to Seton Lake Dam.

Ministry of Environment,
Kamloops 374-9717

# 100 Mile Marsh

*The mallard is the most abundant and widely distributed duck in B.C., occurring virtually everywhere water is present.*

This 20-acre wetland marsh, surrounded by grassy meadows and forested bluffs of white spruce and aspen, is a haven for waterfowl. Located in the heart of the town of 100 Mile House, this site provides easy access for viewing marsh fauna. Canada geese and several species of diving and dabbling ducks nest here. In late spring and early summer it is a good location for viewing waterfowl broods. The wetland also supports muskrats which use the cattail

*Dragonflies are common around marsh and wetland areas where they gorge themselves on mosquitoes and other flying insects.*

habitat for feeding and for building their lodges. While walking around the periphery of the marsh you are bound to find toads, frogs, salamanders and a variety of invertebrate life including dragonflies, water boatmen and freshwater shrimp. Many species of insects and aquatic invertebrates can be discovered throughout spring, summer and fall when numerous songbirds, many of which feed on the abundant insect life, can be seen skimming along the water in search of their prey.

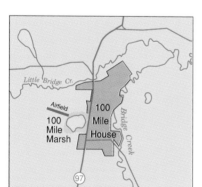

**Directions:** Drive to 100 Mile House on Highway 97. The marsh is on the west side of the highway beside the tourist information booth.

Tourist Information Centre,
100 Mile House 395-5353
Ministry of Environment,
Williams Lake 398-4530

*CENTRAL INTERIOR*

# Scout Island Nature Centre

Williams Lake is a prominent staging area for migrating waterfowl and marsh birds, and provides exceptional viewing opportunities in the spring and fall. An attractive group of islands at the west end of the lake form the Scout Island Nature Centre. Nesting waterfowl, including cinnamon teals and Barrow's goldeneyes raise their broods here during summer months. The brightly coloured yellow-headed blackbirds spread their song throughout the marsh. Between April and July numerous butterflies inhabit the site. Beavers commonly swim next to the lakeshore, and mink are sometimes seen searching for food in the evening and early morning. The crafty red fox is another common resident. It can often be seen sneaking along the shoreline attempting to catch unsuspecting birds or prowling the grassy meadows in search of mice. For all its abundant wildlife, this viewing site is only a few minutes drive from downtown Williams Lake.

Yellow-headed blackbirds nest over water in a basket-like nest which is woven into the emergent vegetation.

Swallowtails are one of the largest types of butterflies. Their colourful wings are large in proportion to their body size.

Another interesting place to explore is the system of trails along Williams Lake River, which flows from Scout Island Marsh through 12 km of scenic valley to the Fraser River.

**Directions:** Drive 1 km southeast of the intersection of Highways 20 and 97 on the seaplane base road.

Ministry of Environment,
Williams Lake 398-4530

# Junction Wildlife Management Area

Over 500 California bighorn sheep inhabit the steep river canyons, forested gullies and dry grassland plateaux, both here and in the neighbouring Farewell Canyon. The site is located at the confluence of the Fraser and Chilcotin rivers, where sagebrush, cactus, balsamroot, and several species of grass cover the plateau. The vegetation on the south slopes becomes green in the spring, consequently attracting mule deer, black bears, coyotes, cougars, snowshoe hares, and a host of other species. Resident sharp-tailed grouse and migrant long-billed curlews are found in the grasslands. Red-tailed hawks and other birds of prey frequently soar in the air overhead. Access to the management area is by four-wheel drive, mountain bike or hiking. However, as it is closed to vehicles between December and March, consider visiting Farewell Canyon, which is open year round.

J. YOUDS

MINISTRY OF ENVIRONMENT

*Predators of California bighorn sheep include coyote, which take many of the young lambs, and cougar, which often kill the solitary rams.*

When viewing bighorn sheep, stay at least 500 m away to avoid stressing the animals, especially during lambing season in April and May.

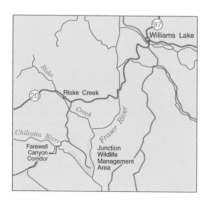

**Directions:** Drive to 1.5 km east of Riske Creek on Highway 20, then 15 km south on South Chilcotin Forestry Road. Turn left to access a public trail into the Wildlife Management Area (11 km) or continue on to Farewell Canyon.

Ministry of Environment,
Williams Lake 398-4530

# Chilanko Marsh WMA*

*As parasitic nesters, redhead ducks will lay their eggs in the nests of other waterfowl and avoid raising their own young.*

This wetland in the middle of the dry interior plateau offers exciting opportunities for viewing migrating waterfowl including teals, pintails, and several species of diving ducks. Barrow's goldeneye and Canada geese are commonly seen nesting here in the summer. You may also see sandhill cranes and Bonaparte's gulls. Beavers and muskrats are common aquatic residents. Beaver trails, cut tree areas and muskrat houses provide viewing opportunities for these animals during spring, summer and fall. American kestrels, eagles and several other birds of prey frequent the marsh, which also supports butterflies, dragonflies and other invertebrates.

Neighbouring upland pine forests, grasslands and pockets of willow and aspen support three-toed woodpeckers, mountain bluebirds, sharp-tailed grouse and many other birds. The area supports a small population of moose in the winter months. Mule deer visit the site throughout the year.

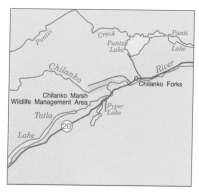

**Directions:** Drive 184 km west of Williams Lake on Highway 20 to Chilanko Forks. Turn north onto Puntzi Mtn. Rd., drive 1.5 km, then turn on Puntzi Airstrip Rd. and drive 2 km.

Ministry of Environment, Williams Lake 398-4530

*Wildlife Management Area

# Horsefly River

The Horsefly River meanders through a picturesque forest valley of cottonwood, red osier and wild rose. This river is a beautiful location for viewing sockeye salmon spawning in the natural river course and in the man-made spawning channels. These run on both sides of the road just south of the town of Horsefly. Watch for schools of these crimson-coloured salmon in pools at the bottom of riffles in August and September. Kokanee also spawn here during September and October and can be seen from the bridge on the Little Horsefly River.

During the spawning season, eagles often perch in the tall cottonwood trees bordering the river to feed on fish carcasses while American dippers, mergansers and other waterfowl are commonly seen on the river as they feed on the salmon eggs.

*A female sockeye salmon will lay up to 4,000 eggs. Only a few young, however, will complete their life cycle and return to spawn.*

Wild rose

**Directions:** Drive northeast of 150 Mile House to Horsefly then east of Horsefly for 1.5 km. Camping is available near Horsefly.

Ministry of Environment,
Williams Lake 398-4530
Fisheries and Oceans,
Quesnel River Hatchery 790-2266

*CENTRAL INTERIOR*

# SOUTHERN INTERIOR MOUNTAINS

Vast mountain ranges cradle deep valleys and long narrow waterways creating a great diversity of climate and habitat in this region. The extensive bodies of water, especially the Columbia River Marshes and the Kootenay River Delta provide important staging areas for migratory birds like tundra swan and Canada geese. The highest breeding concentrations of osprey in the world occur here. Large populations of mountain goat live throughout the mountains, while the diverse forests provide a variety of habitat for grizzly and black bear, mule deer, white-tailed deer, elk, caribou, bighorn sheep and numerous species of small mammals including Columbian ground squirrel and marten.

Black numbers refer to the page numbers of wildlife viewing sites.

# Pend d'Oreille Valley

Mule deer can be recognized by their stiff-legged gait. They bound away using all four legs at once.

The Pend d'Oreille is one of the richest wildlife habitats in the Kootenays. The low, south-facing slopes and mature Douglas fir forests provide excellent winter habitats for white-tailed deer. These animals often

Mountain bluebirds are most common above 1500 m. They often hover low over the ground in search of insects.

congregate near the access road to the Seven Mile Dam. Mule deer are abundant here in the summer while coyote reside in the area year round. Yellow-bellied marmots and ground squirrels scurry about the rocks and grassy meadows in late spring and summer, and ruffed grouse are commonly seen in wooded areas. Eagles gather here in the winter, while in the summer, turkey vultures and osprey can be seen soaring overhead. Western blue-birds and western tanagers are two of the many songbirds that enchant this valley with their lyrical songs where, in the spring and early summer, mountain slopes bloom with wildflowers.

This is the only location in B.C. outside of the Okanagan where you can see praying mantis. Late August and September are the best months to look for these unique insects.

**Directions:** Drive SE of Trail on Hwy 22A to Waneta or south of Salmo on Hwy 6 to Nelway. Follow signs to the Seven Mile Dam.

Ministry of Environment, Nelson 354-6333

# Lower Arrow Lake / Syringa Creek P. P.*

The mixed forests and grasslands on the north slopes of the southern end of Lower Arrow Lake support sizeable populations of ungulates. Rocky Mountain bighorn sheep forage on hillsides along Broadwater Road throughout the year. Elk, white-tailed and mule deer range here in spring; they are best viewed in the mid-afternoon. The early mornings of winter are best for viewing the mountain goats which inhabit the northern aspects of Robson Ridge. The mixed ponderosa pine/Douglas-fir forests and rocky outcrops here also support a diversity of bird life. White-throated swifts nest in the cliffs west of Syringa Creek Park and canyon wrens nest in the canyons near Syringa Creek. While blue and ruffed grouse are common upland residents Canada geese, Barrow's goldeneyes and mergansers are commonly seen on the lake below. The lake can be accessed by boat launches and marinas at the park and by the town of Robson.

*The northern alligator lizard is a diurnal species that prefers cool climates. It feeds throughout the day on insects and small snails.*

Garter snakes, northern alligator lizards and western skinks are common inhabitants of the slopes around Syringa Creek.

* Provincial Park

**Directions:** Drive east of Castlegar across the Kootenay River. Turn north on Highway 6, proceed for 5 km and turn west towards Robson.

Ministry of Environment, Nelson 354-6333

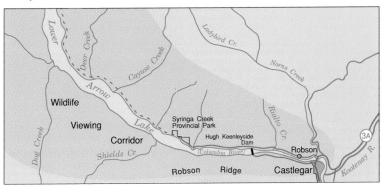

# Kokanee Creek Provincial Park

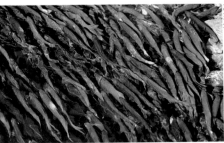

M. NAGA

A. GRASS

*Kokanee are actually landlocked sockeye salmon, spending their entire life in freshwater. They are much smaller than the sea run sockeye.*

*The vocalization of the red squirrel is a long drawn-out chatter. It is most active in summer but does show its face on warm winter days.*

Kokanee Creek flows through a steep canyon bordered by the Douglas fir, western hemlock and pine forests of the Selkirk Mountains to form an alluvial fan and delta where it meets Kootenay Lake. The lake is famous for its record-breaking size kokanee. Large numbers of these brilliantly coloured fish spawn in Kokanee Creek between mid-August and late-September. The banks of this creek provide exceptional opportunities for viewing these fish as well as rainbow and cutthroat trout which also spawn here.

The rich soils and varied climate in this part of the province result in a diversity of habitats that attract coyotes, mule deer, white-tailed deer, squirrels and a host of bird and plant species. Many birds, including hummingbirds and bald eagles, pass through the park. Its year-round residents include pileated woodpeckers, American dippers, and belted kingfishers. Beavers and muskrats live in the creek and the surrounding marshy areas.

A visitor centre next to the Sandspit Campground will provide information on trails and the natural and cultural history of the park.

**Directions:** Drive 20 km east of Nelson on Hwy 3A. Cross the Kokanee Creek bridge and turn right into the park.

Ministry of Environment, Nelson, 354-6333
Ministry of Parks, Nelson 352-5511

# Hill Creek

Hill Creek, which is in the interior cedar/hemlock forest zone, flows through large stands of western red cedar, hemlock, spruce and fir. It provides excellent opportunities for viewing the thousands of kokanee that return to the river each fall to spawn. Black bears, osprey, eagles and other fish-eaters, such as mink and otter, congregate along the river during the kokanee spawning season. In early morning and at dusk, white-tailed and mule deer are fre-

B.C. PARKS

*Chipmunks are kept busy throughout the summer and fall stuffing their cheeks with seeds and other food to store in their winter burrows.*

quently observed moving down to the creek to drink the clear, clean water. American dippers and belted kingfishers are two of the many resident bird species commonly seen along the creek. The nearby Hill Creek hatchery and spawning channels offer easy access to watch the kokanee and learn more about their life cycle. The hatchery is open to the public year round.

*American dipper*

**Directions:** Drive 60 km north of Nakusp. The site is 2 km off Hwy 31. Signs on Hwys 23 and 31 mark the site.

Ministry of Environment,
Nelson 354-6333

# Gerrard

The largest rainbow trout in the world, which can grow to 16 kg in weight, come to spawn in the waters of the Lardeau River, to the south of the clear blue waters of Trout Lake. Up to 1,000 of these giant fish return to the river annually during the month of May. The Lardeau River Valley is a scenic forested corridor where mixed coniferous and deciduous forests provide habitats for white-tailed and mule deer, elk, moose, bears, small mammals and a variety of birds. Grouse and snipe are common in the uplands while coots, Canada geese and a host of other waterfowl are frequently seen along the lakeshore.

Bridge crossings and a viewing platform provide excellent sites for viewing the impressive rainbow trout and other fish such as bull trout, whitefish and kokanee. Kokanee spawn here in late August and September.

*In the late 1950's, due to collection of eggs for transplants, the number of spawning rainbow trout had dropped to fifty fish. The run is now 1,000 fish.*

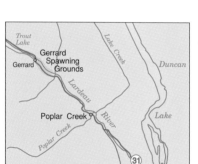

**Directions:** Drive 85 km north of Kaslo on Highway 31 to the old town of Gerrard.

Ministry of Environment, Nelson 354-6333

     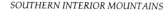

# Creston Valley Wildlife Management Area

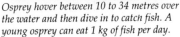
*Osprey hover between 10 to 34 metres over the water and then dive in to catch fish. A young osprey can eat 1 kg of fish per day.*

This internationally-recognized wetland provides staging and nesting areas for thousands of migratory birds on the Pacific Flyway. Over 240 bird species have been recorded in this lush and diverse habitat. The colours, smells, sounds and species of the region change with the seasons. The chatter of large flocks of swans and geese descends on the marsh during spring and fall and thousands of tundra swans visit during March and April. Summer is a time of new plant growth, blossoming wildflowers and broods of young waterfowl. Cavity nesting birds are particularly common and birds of prey can be seen soaring overhead. Osprey can be seen in their large nests or hovering over creeks, looking for fish. White-tailed deer wander through the marsh all year-round and coyotes regularly search for food in the open meadows. The extensive trail system, boardwalks and viewing towers enhance the viewing opportunities here. Visit the interpretive centre for directions to the many access points located throughout the marsh.

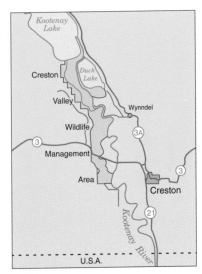

**Directions:** Drive 2 km north of Creston on Highway 3. Turn west, drive 7 km and follow signs to the interpretive centre.

Ministry of Environment, Cranbrook 426-1450
Creston Valley Wildlife Management Area, Creston 428-3260 or 428-3259

# Elko

The dry interior forest zone on the western slopes of the Rocky Mountains is characterized by stands of Douglas fir, ponderosa and lodgepole pine. The mixture of forest and dry, open bunchgrass and fescue grasslands produces an exceptional habitat for Rocky Mountain bighorn sheep, white-tailed and mule deer and mountain goats, especially during winter when the surrounding range is covered with a heavy snowpack. The upper slopes of Mount Broadwood, which rises to the southeast of the highway are good places to look for mountain goats in the spring, summer and fall. The low slopes along Highway 3, just east of the town, are likely places to see bighorn sheep, particularly in the early morning and at dusk. Deer are most abundant here in the winter months, but can still be seen throughout the year.

PROVINCE OF BRITISH COLUMBIA

T. W. HALL

*Rocky Mountain bighorn sheep are active during daylight hours and rest during the night, usually bedding down in the same location.*

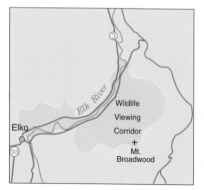

Wildlife Viewing Corridor

+ Mt. Broadwood

Elk River

Elko

SERVICE FACILITIES ARE AVAILABLE AT ELKO AND FERNIE

**Directions:** Drive east of Cranbrook or south of Fernie to Elko. The viewing area stretches 15 km along Highway 3 north of Elko.

Ministry of Environment, Cranbrook 426-1450

*SOUTHERN INTERIOR MOUNTAINS*

# Premier Lake Provincial Park

*Columbian ground squirrels are colonial mammals that are commonly seen in spring and summer but then hibernate for 7-8 months of the year.*

This beautiful park, nestled in the Kootenay Trench, contains several tranquil mountain lakes surrounded by forests of Douglas fir, larch, cottonwood and aspen. Staple Creek, to the south of Premier Lake, is an excellent location to watch rainbow trout spawning in May and June. Osprey and eagles are commonly seen along the creek during these months. Great blue herons, kingfishers and several species of waterfowl are also found throughout the lakes.

An inviting system of trails winds through the area. The park's diverse forest habitat attracts a multitude of forest birds and small mammals such as Columbian ground squirrels. Outside the park, nearby Premier Ridge provides winter range for elk, deer and bighorn sheep which are commonly seen at salt licks on the hillsides west of Canuck Lake. Wild roses, tiger lilies and other wildflowers ornament the park's scenic landscape.

*Belted kingfisher*

Trout eggs are collected here each year and are used to stock lakes throughout B.C.

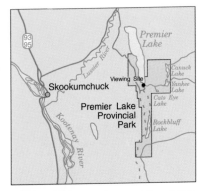

**Directions:** Drive 1.5 km north of Skookumchuck on Highway 95/93 then east 7 km. Turn south 7.5 km to park entrance.

Ministry of Parks, Wasa 422-3212
Ministry of Environment, Cranbrook 426-1450

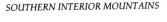

# Kikomun Creek Provincial Park

B.C. PARKS

Kikomun Creek Provincial Park is a prime example of the dry environment of the Rocky Mountain Trench. Its open grasslands, coloured with wild-flowers during spring and summer, are dotted with solitary ponderosa pines, Douglas firs and stands of western larch, lodgepole pine and aspen. These grasslands are a favourite place for deer and elk in the winter months, while yellow pine chipmunks and Columbian ground squirrels scurry about in the summer. Within the park, six warm kettle lakes, remnants from glaciation, provide a home for western painted turtles, which are often seen floating in shallow water or sunning on logs. Barrow's goldeneye, osprey and red-tailed hawks are a few of the many birds to be seen here.

Just north of the park, Kikomun Creek flows into Lake Kookanusa. In September, the creek's clear waters turn red as 10,000-50,000 kokanee move upstream to spawn. The road crossing the creek north of Kikomun Creek Provincial Park provides a good location for viewing them. Watch for bears when hiking along the creek.

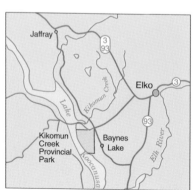

**Directions:** Drive 12 km west of Elko or 16 km south of Jaffray. Watch for B.C. parks signs on Highways 3 and 93.

Ministry of Parks,
Wasa 422-3212
Ministry of Environment,
Invermere 342-4266

*SOUTHERN INTERIOR MOUNTAINS*

# Columbia Wetlands

Bordered by the Rocky and Purcell montains, the Columbia River meanders north from its headwaters in Columbia Lake and forms a vast 26,000 hectare wetland, stretching between Golden and Canal Flats. Spectacular expanses of marsh, river and woodland habitats cover the floor of the Rocky Mountain Trench and support populations of many types of wild-

PROVINCE OF BRITISH COLUMBIA

life, including the majority of the wintering elk in the Columbia River Basin. Moose and deer are common throughout the year and large concentrations of waterfowl, including tundra and trumpeter swans, pass through the area during their spring and fall migrations. Numerous species of songbirds and waterfowl are summer residents. Eagles are most apparent in October, when the kokanee spawn in the creeks and tributaries. Listen for the call of great horned owls in the evenings and watch for coyotes, beavers and great blue herons, which are found all through the wetlands.

P. GEHLEN

*Great horned owls can be recognized by their distinct ear tufts and large size. They hunt at night and can be seen roosting in trees during the day.*

Canoe and float trips are the best ways to explore these wetlands. Campsites and several viewpoints are located along the Highway 95 corridor.

**Directions:** Drive south of Golden or north of Canal Flats on Highway 95. Access the river from side roads off the highway.

Ministry of Environment, Invermere 342-4266

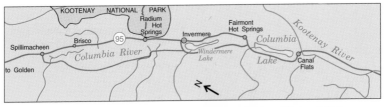

# Kootenay National Park

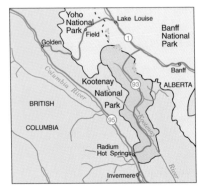

This spectacular mountain park is the only park in B.C. which contains both glaciers and cacti. This diversity in habitat creates an environment which supports 192 bird, 58 mammal, 4 amphibian, 3 reptile and 993 plant species—a multitude of possibilities for wildlife viewing. In spring and early summer, the mountain slopes are covered with western wood lilies, twin flowers and a myriad of other wildflowers. Herds of Rocky Mountain bighorn sheep and elk are frequently seen in spring, summer and fall while mule deer, mountain goats and black bears can be found in the alpine meadows down to the low grasslands.

Rosy finches, Townsend's warblers and pileated woodpeckers are a few of the many bird species which can be seen here. Watch for bats around campground lights in the evening. Visit the park naturalist to find out where to search for rubber boa snakes, wood frogs and long-toed salamanders. Interpretive brochures, checklists and maps are available at the park headquarters.

*The Rocky Mountain bull elk will assemble a herd of up to 60 females. After breeding, however, the bulls leave to join other males.*

**Directions:** Drive west of Banff or north of Invermere to Radium Hot Springs. The park borders Highway 93 between Radium and the Alberta border.

National Parks Service,
Radium Hot Springs 347-9615

*SOUTHERN INTERIOR MOUNTAINS*

# Wells Gray Provincial Park

Spectacular waterfalls, alpine meadows and diverse forests create a magnificent setting for viewing black bear and moose, two of the parks most common residents. The park also supports populations of mule deer, caribou, pine marten, beavers, grizzly bears and wolves. During winter, moose gather around Green Mountain. Bears graze along the roadsides in spring. This is also a good time to see migrating warblers and osprey—only a fraction of the 218 species of birds that have been recorded in the park. Bears feed on fish from August through October, when 4,000-6,000 chinook salmon spawn in the Clearwater River. From a viewing platform at Bailey's Chute you can watch 20 kg salmon leaping up the rapids. Grouse, squirrels, and yellow chipmunks are frequently seen at campsites and along forest trails. Interpretive displays at the park entrance and the information centre in Clearwater will provide details on the best wildlife viewing areas within the park.

MINISTRY OF ENVIRONMENT

*The spruce grouse, also called the "Fool Hen," has little fear of humans and can be approached easily.*

*Moose are usually solitary during summer but will gather in herds in the lowlands during winter.*

Use extreme caution around bears as these animals are unpredictable and potentially dangerous.

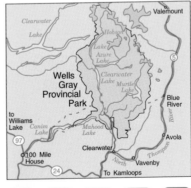

**Directions:** Drive north from Kamloops to Clearwater and continue on. The road follows the Clearwater River corridor into the park.

Ministry of Parks, Clearwater 587-6150
Ministry of Parks, Kamloops 828-4494

# Bowron Lake Provincial Park

PROVINCE OF BRITISH COLUMBIA

This chain of lakes, marshes and rivers winds through gentle mountain slopes. Canoeists praise this 116 km looping waterway as a scenic and wildlife wonder. Moose are most commonly seen in the early morning or at dusk in the marshy southwest corner of the circuit. Look for them around Unna, Babcock and Spectacle lakes and near the Bowron Slough. Beavers live throughout the lakes and build their lodges and dams along the waterways. The call of the loon can often be heard ringing across the lakes. Several species of waterfowl nest here while others migrate through in spring and fall. Osprey are frequently seen diving for fish or sitting on large nests which are usually perched on top of dead trees. Grouse are common in the forest. Black bears are often seen in the evening or early morning along the lakeshores, so make sure to hang

L. HALVERSON

*Grizzly bears are usually solitary animals but during salmon runs they often congregate in small groups along the river.*

your food in the trees when camping. The best time to visit this area is between the months of June and September. An information centre at the park entrance will provide directions for trips of varying lengths. Access to this world famous site is by canoe only.

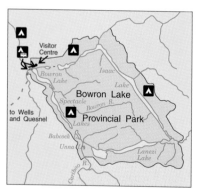

During late summer and fall, grizzly bears move to the Upper Bowron River to take advantage of spawning salmon. To avoid human/bear conflicts, access to the river is restricted during this period.

**Directions:** Drive north to Quesnel and turn east on Highway 26 to Wells. Follow the secondary road 29 km northeast to the park entrance.

Ministry of Parks, Williams Lake 398-4414

*SOUTHERN INTERIOR MOUNTAINS*

# Cranberry Marsh

An abundance of upland cover and an expanse of marsh habitat make this site a haven for waterfowl and other wildlife. Ducks Unlimited has enhanced the site with nesting islands, open waterways and water control structures. The marsh is an exceptionally productive area for waterfowl, and also supports populations of mule deer, moose, bear and a variety of small mammals. Canada geese and many other water birds nest in the marsh, while numerous species of songbirds inhabit the upland shrub and forest lands. Northern harriers and red-tailed hawks are two of the many raptors commonly seen over the marsh. A network of trails and observation towers offer exceptional viewing opportunities.

*Red-winged blackbirds are very territorial nesters. In spring, the males arrive prior to the females to stake out a nest site.*

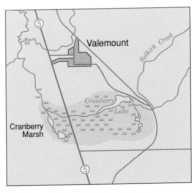

**Directions:** Drive 3 km south of Valemount on Highway 5. Take the road S.E. of Valemount for 4 km to Cranberry Lake.

Ministry of Environment,
Prince George 565-6145

# Rearguard Falls Provincial Park

By the time the chinook salmon reach Rearguard Falls they have travelled over 1,200 kilometres from the Strait of Georgia.

Surrounded by scenic Rocky Mountain vistas, these falls are set among white spruce and subalpine fir forest. They are the final barrier to the migrating salmon which have travelled 1,200 km up the Fraser River from the Pacific Ocean. A lookout provides a good vantage point to spot the large chinook salmon leaping into the air as they attempt to make their way up the impassable, ten-metre high falls. The salmon enter the Fraser River near Vancouver in early July and arrive at Rearguard Falls during August and September. Unable to swim above the falls, the salmon spawn in the stretches of river just downstream. American dippers can be seen along the river as they search for salmon eggs. Several species of songbirds are found in the surrounding forests.

**Directions:** Drive east of Prince George on Highway 16. Turn south off Hwy 16, 4.5 km east of Tête Jaune Cache.

Ministry of Parks,
Prince George 565-6340
Ministry of Parks,
Valemount 566-4325

# Mount Robson Provincial Park

Within this scenic mountain park, the headwaters of the Fraser River flow past Mount Robson, the highest peak in the Canadian Rockies. Here, a diversity of forest types, majestic alpine meadows, mountain lakes and rivers offer an extraordinarily scenic backdrop to a host of wildlife viewing opportunities. During spring and summer, the south end of Moose Lake, and the marsh along the Fraser River south of Moose River provide exceptional opportunities to watch moose, elk, deer, black bears, beavers, muskrats and mink. Common loons, red-necked grebes and several species of waterfowl and shorebirds also spend the summer in this lake and marsh sanctuary while numerous species of songbirds can be seen throughout the park's upland areas. Paddling through the marsh is a great way to experience many of its wonders. The interpretive centre at the western entrance to the park is a good place to obtain directions to the many viewing sites throughout the park.

*Red-necked grebes nest in small colonies on freshwater lakes and marshes throughout B.C. and winter in quiet waters along the coast.*

In the spring, watch for grizzly bears and mountain goats along the rock slide areas on the north side of the Yellowhead Highway.

**Directions:** Drive east of Prince George on Highway 16 towards Jasper. Drive 25 km east of the park entrance on to Moose Lake Marsh.

Ministry of Parks,
Prince George 565-6340

# SUB-BOREAL INTERIOR

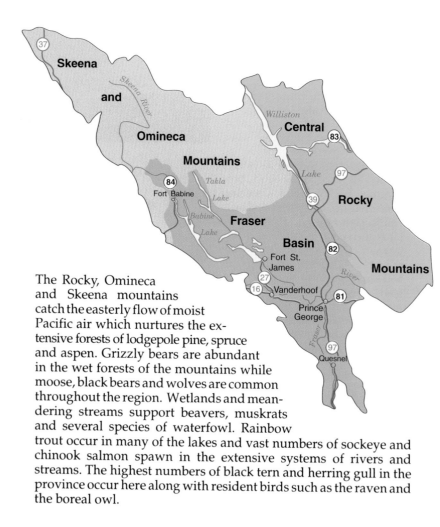

The Rocky, Omineca and Skeena mountains catch the easterly flow of moist Pacific air which nurtures the extensive forests of lodgepole pine, spruce and aspen. Grizzly bears are abundant in the wet forests of the mountains while moose, black bears and wolves are common throughout the region. Wetlands and meandering streams support beavers, muskrats and several species of waterfowl. Rainbow trout occur in many of the lakes and vast numbers of sockeye and chinook salmon spawn in the extensive systems of rivers and streams. The highest numbers of black tern and herring gull in the province occur here along with resident birds such as the raven and the boreal owl.

Black numbers refer to the page numbers of wildlife viewing sites.

# Tabor Mountain

*Moose are attracted to disturbed sites such as old burns and cleared areas where fresh shrub growth provides abundant browse.*

In 1961, a spectacular fire blazed through the Grove Forest just east of Prince George, burning over 26,000 hectares and leaving a scorched landscape with pockets of unburned standing timber throughout the site. The natural process of forest succession has since resulted in a deciduous forest of willow and alder which provides excellent habitat for many types of wildlife. Large numbers of moose winter here to take cover in the tall stands of willow and to forage on younger vegetation. Wolves and coyotes, which feed on the moose and deer, are often heard howling at night and are occasionally seen wandering through clearings. Other resident species include lynx, snowshoe hare, beaver, black bear and several raptor species.

In the spring and summer, the willow thickets are filled with the songs and calls of a multitude of songbirds. An observation tower offers a great location for wildlife viewing.

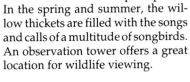

*Snowshoe hare*

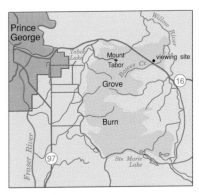

**Directions:** Drive 30 km east of Prince George on Highway 16. A sign on the highway identifies the pull-out.

Ministry of Environment,
Prince George 565-6135

# Crooked River

K. CHILD

*Up to 70 trumpeter swans winter along the Crooked River. This is their most northerly wintering site in B.C.'s interior.*

PROVINCE OF BRITISH COLUMBIA

Stretches of open water along the meandering Crooked River attract one of the few wintering populations of trumpeter swans found in central B.C. These rare and beautiful birds reside here through the winter months and migrate to their nesting grounds in the far north in the spring. The open water here also attracts other overwintering birds such as Barrow's goldeneye, American dipper and belted kingfisher.

In summer, the neighbouring lowlands contain small lakes, ponds and wet meadows which provide food and cover for beavers, muskrats, otters, black bears and moose. Canoeing along this gently flowing waterway is a perfect way to view these riparian inhabitants. In spring and fall, you'll hear the calls and chatter of flocks of migrating waterfowl and songbirds that frequent this productive river habitat. Camping facilities are available at nearby Crooked River Provincial Park.

As many as 70 swans have been seen wintering along the Crooked River. These birds should be viewed from a distance to avoid unnecessarily disturbing them.

**Directions:** Drive 85 km north of Prince George on Highway 97. River access is on the west side of the highway.

Ministry of Environment,
Prince George 565-6135

*SUB-BOREAL INTERIOR*

# Dunlevy Creek

The landscape surrounding Dunlevy Creek consists of a unique combination of habitats, including aspen parkland, boreal forest and alpine fir. The area sustains significant numbers of large ungulates, including stone sheep, deer, elk, moose and caribou. A 7 km hike will take you to Butler Ridge, where you can see resident populations of stone sheep, ptarmigan, and ruffed, spruce and blue grouse. During winter months, Rocky Mountain elk graze on low, open slopes while deer and moose commonly feed in the shrub and grassland habitats along road 190. Dinosaur Lake and the ranges north of the W.A.C. Bennett Dam are good locations for viewing a variety of birds and large mammals.

During summer, several species of songbirds inhabit the forests. Chipmunks, squirrels and marmots can be seen throughout the area. Access to much of the area is by hiking the scenic forest trails and open alpine ridgetops.

*Being primarily nocturnal animals, white-tailed deer usually bed down at dawn and become active again in the late afternoon and early evening.*

*Golden eagle*

**Directions:** Drive north of Chetwynd or west of Fort St. John to Hudson's Hope, then west on Road #520 to W.A.C. Bennett Dam.

Ministry of Environment, Fort St. John, 787-3295

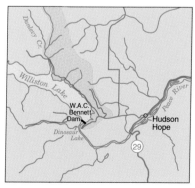

# Babine River

*The black bear is an opportunistic feeder that looks clumsy when it walks but it can reach speeds of 50 km per hour in short bursts.*

This pristine wilderness river flows through forests of spruce, pine and aspen in its eastern reaches. To the west, where the Babine meets the Skeena River, cedar, hemlock and Douglas fir cover the mountain slopes. The Babine is one of the most productive salmon spawning rivers in the ecoprovince. A road north of Fort Babine provides access to the site where the sockeye spawn between mid-August and October. Access to most of this scenic river is by whitewater boat, but a 6 km trail on the east side of the river, downstream of Nilkitkwa Lake, allows you to walk along the river. Here, grizzly and black bears, deer and moose are often seen. Moose are most common between the river corridor between October and April on south facing slopes and bears inhabit the river corridor between August and October to feed on salmon.* Gulls, eagles, ravens and mergansers are other common sites along the river, especially during the spawning season.

Moose

*Use extreme caution around grizzly or black bears or in bear habitat. They are unpredictable and potentially dangerous animals.

**Directions:** Drive 126 km north of Smithers to the bridge crossing at the outlet of Nilkitkwa Lake.

Ministry of Environment, Smithers 847-7303

# NORTHERN BOREAL MOUNTAINS

This northern landscape contains some of the largest expanses of wilderness in B.C. The climate ranges from extreme cold and frequent snow storms in winters to mild and humid in summers. The topography varies from high rugged mountains with narrow valleys to rolling mountains and plateaus intersected by wide valleys. Caribou, thinhorn sheep and moose best characterize the fauna of this remote area. Grizzly bears, black bears and wolves are common throughout the valleys of low scrub and wetlands while mountain goats are abundant in the rugged alpine areas. This is the centre of concentration for Bohemian waxwings and willow and rock ptarmigan. Many species including the Pacific loon, gyrfalcon and snow bunting breed nowhere else in the province.

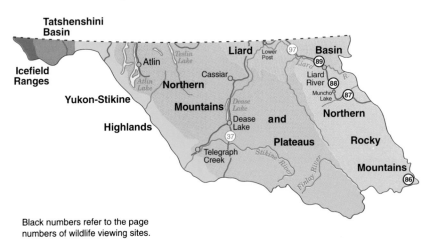

Black numbers refer to the page numbers of wildlife viewing sites.

# Pink Mountain

In the early summer a profusion of wildflowers form a colourful mantle on the picturesque foothills of the Rocky Mountains. The boreal, subalpine and alpine habitats on Pink Mountain are home to caribou, moose, mule deer, white-tailed deer and elk. The lowlands to the north and west sides of the mountain are the only places in the province where you can see wild plains bison. Caribou, a permanent resident, can be seen on the mountain top in the summer. Moose live in the shrub and grassland areas at the south end of the mountain and in the lowlands to the east and west. Grizzly and black bears are also common residents and you may even hear wolves howling in the evenings. Three species of ptarmigan live in the alpine habitat, while ruffed and spruce grouse inhabit the boreal forest. Hawks, owls and a variety of songbirds, including bohemian waxwings and horned larks, nest in this captivating landscape.

A. GRASS

B.C. PARKS / GRANT

*Plains bison were reintroduced into this area in the late 1970s. Their numbers have been growing steadily ever since.*

*During the mid-summer heat, when insects are out in full force, caribou can be found on snow patches where they gather to avoid the bugs.*

A unique feature of this site is the several species of arctic butterflies which abound during the summer months.

**Directions:** Drive 16 km north of Fort St. John on the Alaska Highway, turn west at mile 147 on Road #192 for 16 km and take the north fork to the top of the mountain.

Ministry of Environment,
Fort St. John 787-3295

# Stone Mountain Provincial Park

The Alaska Highway winds through the breathtaking northern Rocky Mountains, where alpine meadows bloom with wildflowers in July. This park offers several locations for viewing moose, mule deer, black bears and impressive herds of stone sheep which are commonly seen here in the summer months. In the fall, woodland caribou frequent the highway corridor; between June and September they reside in the alpine areas. Throughout the year, in the early morning and evening, moose are common in the lowland spruce habitats. Black bears can be found in the subalpine region in July and August. The Flower Springs Lake trail is a good place to see wildflowers and a host of wildlife species including ptarmigan, grouse, harlequin ducks and several species of songbirds.

*PROVINCE OF BRITISH COLUMBIA*

*B.C. PARKS*

*The dark-coloured stone sheep are a southern subspecies of Dall sheep. More northern populations are grey to white in colour.*

In addition to many wildlife viewing opportunities, the park offers spectacular landscape features such as the 100 metre high hoodoos at Wokkpash Creek.

**Directions:** Drive 160 km west of Fort Nelson on the Alaska Highway.

Ministry of Parks,
Fort St. John 787-3407

# Muncho Lake Provincial Park

B. WAREHAM

*Both parents of the common loon incubate their eggs. The family deserts the nest soon after the young hatch. Chicks often hitch a ride on their parents' back.*

This northern park is located among the spruce forests and rolling alpine of the Northern Rocky Mountains. Here, open meadows and mineral licks provide unique opportunities for viewing ungulates, birds and wildflowers. Between May and September up to 200 stone sheep range between the southern end of Muncho Lake and the northern boundary of the park. Other residents include moose, caribou, mule deer, grizzlies and black bears. May and June are good months to see caribou in the river valley and moose along the Toad and Trout Rivers.

Muncho Lake is also a staging area for migrating waterfowl. Loons, grebes, Canada geese and mergansers are common here. Resident ptarmigan and spruce grouse are joined by dozens of annual migrant species including nuthatches, hummingbirds and flycatchers. Mid-July is an excellent time to hike through the wildflowers in the alpine meadows.

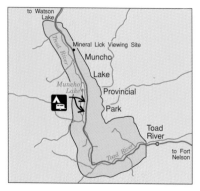

Sheep are attracted to mineral accumulations along the highway and are most active at dawn and dusk in the spring and summer. A natural mineral lick at mile 472 is a good viewing site.

**Directions:** Drive 250 km west of Fort Nelson on the Alaska Highway.

Ministry of Parks,
Fort St. John 787-3407

# Liard River Hotsprings Provincial Park

*Boreal toads are widespread throughout B.C., occurring from sea level to high mountainous areas.*

This park contains lush boreal spruce marshes and the second largest hotsprings system in Canada. The springs produce an extraordinarily warm micro-climate, providing many unique wildlife viewing opportunities. The Liard is often called the "Tropical Valley." Over 250 species of boreal forest plants live here—several because of the influence of the springs. Fourteen species of orchids are found in the park, as are carnivorous plants such as sundew, butterwort and aquatic bladderwort. Many intriguing species of insects live here, and lake chub occur in large numbers in the warm swamps.

This is one of the best locations in the province to observe and photograph moose, common residents between April and October. Look for them feeding in marshy areas in the early mornings and evenings. The area also supports black bears and porcupines. The songs and calls of numerous shorebirds, waterfowl and songbirds enhance the impression of a tropical oasis in this fascinating northern environment.

*Yellow lady's-slipper*

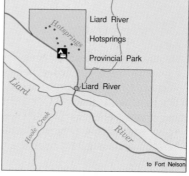

**Directions:** Drive 320 km west of Fort Nelson on the Alaska Highway.

Ministry of Parks,
Fort St. John, 787-3407

*NORTHERN BOREAL MOUNTAINS*

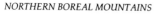

# BOREAL & TAIGA PLAINS

Persistent arctic weather maintains cold winters in the Boreal and Taiga plains of northeastern B.C., while the warm weather and long daylight hours of spring bring these areas to life. These low-profile landscapes may appear sterile, yet many species of wildlife persist through the harsh winter climate.

The Boreal Plains consist of a wide plateau and a lowland plain incised by several rivers. The upland habitat includes muskeg and forests of black and white spruce and lodgepole pine while the broad lowlands of the Peace Valley consist of grasslands, aspen forests and numerous wetlands. Moose, mule deer, and black bear are common in the lowlands while caribou, lynx, wolverine and fisher inhabit the upland forests. This area is the center of abundance for broad-winged hawk, sharp-tailed grouse and Franklin's gull.

The Taiga Plains offer a landscape of muskeg lowlands extending to the Mackenzie Delta. Tamarack and black spruce forests, inhabited by black bear, moose, lynx, snowshoe hares, spruce grouse and meadow jumping mice, are interspersed with pristine wetlands and quiet meandering streams with beaver, muskrat and flocks of waterfowl. B.C.'s largest concentrations of breeding lesser yellowlegs, solitary sandpipers and swamp sparrows are in this region. Scattered herds of caribou spend the winter in the upland muskeg and boreal forest.

**Taiga Plains**

Fort Nelson Lowland Ecoregion

Fort Nelson

**Boreal Plains**

Alberta Plateau Ecoregion

Fort St. John

Hudson's Hope

Dawson Creek

*Snowshoe hare*
*(facing page)*
D. SCHMIDT

# The 50 most sought after wildlife species in B.C. and where to find them

*Probability of viewing:*

**H** - High: Given the right time and location.
**M** - Moderate: No guarantee but likely.
**L** - Low: Unlikely without significant effort.

*The seasons during which you can see the species in B.C.:*

S - spring        S - summer
F - fall          W - winter

\* *Vulnerable, sensitive or unpredictable species. Should be viewed with caution from a safe distance. Avoid disturbing these species.*

**American Dipper**          H    S S F W
Common along mountain streams and rivers. Adams River, Kokanee Creek, Goldstream Park, Hill Creek, Gerrard, Stamp Falls, Coquihalla River.

**American Kestrel**         H    S S F W
Commonly seen on poles and fence posts. Nicola Valley, Tranquille, Columbia Wetlands.

**Bald Eagle**               H    S S F W
Active Pass, Harrison River, Babine River, Skeena River and most other coastal areas and salmon spawning streams.

**Barrow's Goldeneye**       H    S S F W
Breed in central interior, winter along coast. Sidney Spit, Iona Beach, Chilanko Marsh, Reifel Sanctuary, Scout Island and the east coast of Vancouver Island.

**\* Black Bear**            M    S S F W
Creston Valley, Adams River, Wells Gray Park, Mount Robson Park, Bowron Lakes, L. Arrow Lake, Strathcona Park and most northern parks.

**Black Brant**              H    S S F W
Migrate along B.C. Coast in spring. Parksville/Qualicum, Boundary Bay, Reifel Sanctuary, Sidney Spit.

**California Bighorn Sheep** M    S S F W
Inhabit grasslands and mountain slopes in the dry interior. Junction W.M.A., South Thompson River, Vaseux Lake.

**Caribou**                  M    S S F W
Most often found in high elevation and wilderness areas. Pink Mountain, Stone Mtn. Park, Muncho Lk. Park.

**Cinnamon Teal**            M    S S F W
Breed in south and central B.C. Serpentine, Reifel Sanctuary, Nicola Valley, 100 Mile Marsh, Columbia Wetlands.

**Coyote**                   M    S S F W
Often seen in open meadows. Tranquille W.M.A., Serpentine, Creston, Junction W.M.A., Tabor Mtn., Columbia Wetlands, Nicola Valley, Boundary Bay, Osoyoos Oxbows.

**Dunlin**                   L    S S F W
Breed along north coast, winters on south coast. Boundary Bay, Reifel Sanctuary, Courtenay Estuary, Parksville/Qualicum, Delkatla Slough.

**Elk**                      M    S S F W
Higher elevations in summer, lowlands in winter. Kootenay N.P., Columbia Wetlands, Strathcona Park, Kikomun Creek, Dunlevy Creek.

**Golden Eagle**             L    S S F W
Year-round resident in B.C.'s interior. Winter along coast. Dunlevy Creek, Hedley-Keremeos Cliffs, Pend d'Orielle Valley, Wells Gray Park.

**\* Gray Whale**            L    S S F W
Migrate along outer coast, some summer residents along west coast Vancouver Island. French Beach, Pacific Rim N.P.

**Great Blue Heron**         H    S S F W
Common around wetlands and coastal marshes. Reifel Sanctuary, Iona Beach, Boundary Bay, Burnaby Lake, Sidney Spit, Courtenay Estuary, Somenos Marsh, Serpentine Fen, Pitt-Addington W.M.A., Creston W.M.A. and Columbia Wetlands.

**Great Gray Owl**           L    S S F W
Resident throughout most of B.C. Prefers pine and spruce forest habitats. Chilanko Marsh, South Thompson River, Okanagan Falls.

**Great Horned Owl**         L    S S F W
Usually roost in trees during daylight hours. Mission Creek, Creston W.M.A., Adams River, Somenos, Columbia Wetlands.

**\* Grizzly Bear**          L    S S F W
Live in remote wilderness, common around salmon streams in fall. Babine River, Mount Robson Park, Kootenay N.P., Stone Mountain Park, Muncho Lake, Pink Mountain.

**Harlequin Duck**           M    S S F W
Summer along mountain streams and rivers, winters along coast. Iona Beach, Nanaimo Harbour, Parksville/Qualicum, Blackfish Sound, Mitlenatch Island and most northern mountain streams.

**\* Killer Whale**          M    S S F W
Summer throughout the Strait of Georgia and along the B.C. coast. Blackfish Sound, Active Pass, Sidney Spit.

**Kokanee**                  H    S S F W
Live in lakes, spawn in interior mountain streams. Kokanee Cr., Peachland Cr., Mission Cr., Hill Cr., Gerrard.

**Moose**                    M    S S F W
Common throughout the interior and northern regions. Pink Mtn., Muncho Lk., Wells Gray Park, Crooked R., Mount Robson Park, Tabor Mountain, Columbia Wetlands, Liard River Hotsprings, Bowron Lakes, Stone Mtn. Park.

**Mountain Goat**            H    S S F W
Live in alpine areas and rugged mountain terrain. Elko, Hedley/Keremeos, Seton Lake, Kootenay N.P., Lower Skeena River.

**Mule Deer**　　　　H　S S F W
Common throughout B.C., gather in large herds on winter and spring ranges. Lower Arrow Lake, Pend d'Orielle Valley, Columbia Wetlands, Dunlevy Cr., Tranquille, Kikomun Cr., Junction W.M.A., Elko.

**Osprey**　　　　　M　S S F W
Nest near streams, rivers, and lakes. Creston W.M.A., Pitt-Addington W.M.A., Wells Gray Park, Bowron Lakes, Osoyoos Oxbows, South Thompson River.

**Pacific Loon**　　　H　S S F W
Winter along coast, breeds in northern lakes. Active Pass, Courtenay R. Estuary, Blackfish Sound, Nanaimo Harbour, Iona Beach.

**Pelagic Cormorant**　H　S S F W
Nest in large colonies, usually on cliffs. Mitlenatch Island, Active Pass, Blackfish Sound.

**Pika**　　　　　　M　S S F W
Mountain dweller, common at base of tallus slopes. Seton Lake, Kootenay N.P., Manning Park, Coquihalla River.

**Pileated Woodpecker**　M　S S F W
Resident, found in mixed deciduous/coniferous forests. Creston W.M.A., Peachland Cr., Mission Cr., Kokanee Cr.

**Red-tailed Hawk**　　H　S S F W
Common in agricultural and wetland areas. Boundary Bay, Nicola Valley, Swan Lake, Somenos Marsh, Reifel Sanctuary, South Thompson River, Pitt-Addington W.M.A.

**Rocky Mountain Bighorn Sheep**　　H　S S F W
Elko, Kootenay N.P., Lower Arrow Lake, Columbia Wetlands.

**Ruffed Grouse**　　M　S S F W
Common in mixed deciduous/coniferous forests near wetlands. Adams River, Wells Gray Park, Lower Arrow Lake, Strathcona Park, Dunlevy Creek.

**\* Sandhill Crane**　　L　S S F W
Secretive bird, nests in quiet wetland areas. Nicola Valley, Delkatla Slough, Pitt-Addington W.M.A.

**Sea Lion**　　　　M　S S F W
Dispersed along the coast in summer, congregates in large groups in winter on Vancouver Island. Active Pass, Nanaimo Harbour, Blackfish Sound, Pacific Rim N.P.

**Sharp-tailed Grouse**　M　S S F W
Inhabit open grassland in the dry interior. Junction W.M.A., Nicola Valley.

**Short-eared Owl**　　L　S S F W
Common around large open plains and marshes. Boundary Bay, Reifel Sanctuary, Somenos Marsh, Osoyoos Oxbows, Columbia Wetlands, Creston.

**Snow Goose**　　　H　S S F W
Migrate along coast in spring and fall. Reifel Sanctuary, Iona Beach, Boundary Bay, Courtenay Estuary, Parksville/Qualicum.

**Sockeye Salmon**　　H　S S F W
Spawn between September and November. Adams River, Horsefly River, Stamp Falls, Babine River.

**Steelhead**　　　　H　S S F W
Spawn in June and July. Coquihalla River Canyon.

**Stone Sheep**　　　H　S S F W
Most common in alpine areas of northern regions. Stone Mtn. Park, Muncho Lake Park, Dunlevy Creek.

**Tufted Puffin**　　　L　S S F W
Nest on cliffs along outer coast of B.C. and Alaska. Winter all along the west coast. Pacific Rim N.P.

**Trumpeter Swan**　　H　S S F W
Winter along B.C. coast and interior regions. South Thompson River, Crooked River, Somenos Marsh, Courtenay Estuary, Reifel Sanctuary, Nanaimo Harbour.

**Tundra Swan**　　　H　S S F W
Migrate through B.C. in spring and fall. Winters on some interior waterways. Pitt-Addington W.M.A., South Thompson River, Creston, Columbia Wetlands, Courtenay Estuary, Reifel Sanctuary, Tranquille W.M.A.

**\* Western Grebe**　　H　S S F W
Nest in the interior and winters along the coast. Salmon Arm Bay, Creston, Courtenay Estuary, Iona Beach, Parksville/Qualicum.

**Western Painted Turtle**　M　S S F W
Inhabit warm freshwater ponds, lakes and marshes. Swan Lake, Osoyoos Oxbows, Kikomun Creek, Vaseux Lake, Mission Creek, Salmon Arm Bay.

**Western Sandpiper**　M　S S F W
Migrate through B.C. in spring and late summer. Inhabits mud flats and sandy beaches. Boundary Bay, Iona Beach, Courtenay Estuary, Parksville/Qualicum, Pacific Rim N.P., French Beach.

**White-tailed Deer**　M　S S F W
Inhabit mixed forest and open meadows near agricultural land. Pend d'Orielle Valley, Columbia Wetlands, Mission Cr., Lower Arrow Lake, Kikomun Creek, Dunlevy Creek, Creston W.M.A.

**White-tailed Ptarmigan**　M　S S F W
Common in alpine areas. Pink Mountain, Manning Park, Stone Mountain Park, Dunlevy Cr., Muncho Lake.

**Wolf**　　　　　　L　S S F W
Common in wilderness, central and northern areas. Tabor Mtn., Pink Mountain, Stone Mountain Park, Muncho Lake, Wells Gray Park.

**Wood Duck**　　　H　S S F W
Nest in tree cavities, resident in southwestern B.C. Reifel Sanctuary, Somenos Marsh, Burnaby Lake, Pitt-Addington W.M.A., Mission Creek.

# Index